"What a welcome gift this book is to a generation that frequently seems too busy to remember or to cultivate its family and church traditions. Through establishing the origins of the traditions and making the faith connection with them, the authors call us first to reflection and only then to action in the extension activities. *Advent and Lent Activities for Children* will be an excellent resource for teachers and catechists in their classes and in partnership with families."

Sr. Jude Fitzpatrick
Superintendent of Schools
Diocese of Des Moines

"In *Advent and Lent Activities for Children* Shiela Kielly and Sheila Geraghty have created an easily accessible resource of holiday information and activities that is both imaginative and practical. Teachers will love having tidbits about origins, practical ideas for connecting traditional customs and symbols to modern life, and a variety of suggestions for activities for multi-level age groups all in one book. This is a must for busy catechists!"

Carole MacClennan
Author, *When Jesus Was Young* and *Learning by Doing*

"I am looking forward to this wonderfully creative book being in the hands of religious educators. It is a great resource for bringing joy, enthusiasm, and fuller meaning into the journey of faith. I particularly like the section called 'connections' which integrates creative activity with the deeper aspects of our faith."

Joyce Rupp
Des Moines, Iowa

"*Advent and Lent Activities for Children* will delight and inform people of all ages. The authors have found a marvelous balance of information, activity, and prayer. Did you ever wonder why there are Easter rabbits or why cows appear in the Christmas scene? This book is a resource for understanding the rituals and traditions that have become second nature to our celebrations. Added to the historical perspective of the symbols and signs that fill our liturgical seasons, the authors have given catechists, parents, and all Christians, activities to incorporate into each of these rich, symbolic traditions.

"A much needed resource book that will find you engrossed in the reading and excited about the extension activities. It is a gift to purchase for family and friends and recommend to people who minister to families and young people."

Charlotte McCoy
Director of Youth Formation
Archdiocese of Dubuque

Advent & Lent
ACTIVITIES
FOR CHILDREN

Camels
Carols
Crosses
and
Crowns

SHIELA KIELLY   SHEILA GERAGHTY

TWENTY-THIRD PUBLICATIONS
Mystic, CT 06355

Third printing 1997

Twenty-Third Publications
185 Willow Street
P.O. Box 180
Mystic, CT 06355
(860) 536-2611
800-321-0411

ISBN 0-89622-676-X
Library of Congress Catalog Card Number 95-61490
Printed in the U.S.A.

CONTENTS

Advent and Lent Activities for Children

INTRODUCTION

Customs and traditions call us to take a moment, step out of the normal pace of life, and reflect. They help us to remember, to celebrate, and to honor. Celebrating customs and traditions helps us to know who we are, where we came from, who has gone before us, and where we are going.

Camels, Carols, Crosses, Crowns: Advent and Lent Activities for Children explores some of our Christian customs and traditions, particularly those associated with Advent, Christmas, Lent, and Easter. It describes how they evolved in different countries and cultures, and proposes ways that they may be celebrated today.

Each custom and tradition in this book is explored in the following way:

—*Origin* helps us come to an understanding of the history of a particular tradition.

—*Connection* expands a thought or idea from historical roots of a custom or tradition, to a more spiritual dimension.

—*Extension* provides a variety of ways to use the custom or tradition in a classroom, home, parish group, small faith community, or other such setting.

How do customs and traditions get started? Initially, they may have a practical significance that becomes blurred through years as the custom or tradition is incorporated into other cultural practices. In the end, what often remains is the practice without any obvious connection to a point of origin.

Many of our current Christian traditions had their origin in pagan rituals. Ancient peoples created these rituals for many reasons, for example, in response to nature, as protection from evil spirits, or to honor their gods. These cultural practices eventually took on new meaning when adapted for Christian use.

Customs and traditions usually begin in a particular location, moving with people as they go on to other regions. As customs move from place to place, they are often adapted to fit in with the new surroundings, or to the materials that are available there. In the end, the new country may assume ownership of the custom or tradition. For this reason, the beginnings of many customs and traditions can be attributed to a variety of countries.

Some of the information you read in this book may be contradictory to or in dispute with what you have previously heard. Bear in mind that early traditions were orally recalled, and more than one version probably does exist.

Also, let it be known that we, the authors, are not experts on the development and practice of customs and traditions. Rather, we are curious Christians who find meaning in examining our forebears' ways of celebrating holidays, feasts, and the like.

Practicing or creating traditions does not require vast amounts of time, energy, or money. Using the good dishes for the family meal on a member's birthday, on the first day of school, or in honor of an achievement can be a simple, yet meaningful, tradition. Choosing a Christmas tree and putting up the holiday decorations is another common ritual for most people.

Reflect on your relationships and recall the many traditions you already have in place. Are there certain foods you eat, or favorite clothes you wear, for special occasions? Does a relative always bring a particular food to the family picnic? Do you have an annual viewing of a meaningful movie? Is there a special celebration for an elder's birthday? Do you all gather on Christmas Eve or Independence Day?

It is our hope that *Camels, Carols, Crosses, Crowns: Advent and Lent Activities for Children* will inspire your creativity, and encourage you to begin or to revive your own traditions. Through revitalizing our holiday practices, we expand our relationship with God, and come to better know who we are as a Christian people. May great joy and meaning be attached to your celebration of the many customs and traditions available to us today.

ADVENT
&
CHRISTMAS

ADVENT

The word Advent means "coming." Used to describe the time before Christmas, Advent signifies the coming of Jesus in Bethlehem, Jesus' future coming at the end of the world, and his present coming in the hearts of people.

The Council of Tours in 567 set aside a time before Christmas when people were to prepare themselves physically, mentally, and spiritually to celebrate Jesus' birth. The bishop of Tours issued a regulation that a fast should be held throughout Gaul on three days of every week from November 11 (the feast of St. Martin) until Christmas. People were to abstain from wine, ale, honey-beer, meats, fats, cheese, and fatty fish. Fasting also meant no weddings, amusements, pleasure travel, and conjugal relations.

In Rome, the celebration of Advent started during the reign of Pope Gregory the Great (590-604) and lasted through four Sundays. In contrast to the penitential tone observed in Gaul, the Roman Advent was a time of joyful preparation to celebrate the remembrance of Jesus' birth.

Eventually, the contrasting themes of Advent as a season of joy, and Advent as a season of penance, were combined. Today, we observe Advent as a four-week period of spiritual preparation anticipating the birth of Jesus.

CHRISTMAS

Nobody knows precisely where or when Jesus was born. Indeed, the details are not that important; the power of the celebration is that Jesus took on human life, and yet remained God.

It has been theorized that Mary and Joseph made the 100-mile trip from Nazareth to Bethlehem on foot in September or October, before the winter weather set in. (December in that region is known for cold, torrential rains and furious winds.) They were in Bethlehem, along with many other people, to register for a tax.

At the time of Jesus' birth, there were no inns or guest rooms in Bethlehem, although there were in Jerusalem, an hour or two away by foot. Mary and Joseph may have had relatives in Bethlehem with whom they stayed, and Jesus could have been born there. It is also possible that Mary gave birth in a cave in the limestone hills surrounding Bethlehem.

For the first three centuries after Jesus' death, the date of his birth was assigned to various days of the year. Some Christian groups included its celebration on the feast of the Epiphany, rather than marking it with a separate day. In 350, Pope Julius set the date of Christ's birth as December 25, to coincide with the celebration of the winter solstice. At the time this date was determined, a mistake on the Julian calendar showed the winter solstice occurring on the 25th, rather than the 21st, of December.

The pagan celebration of the winter solstice occurred on the shortest day of the year, and served to call back the sun. These ancient festivities had a great deal in common with our modern Christmas customs, including gift giving, decorating with evergreens and lights, and banquets. Also near that time of year, the Hebrew people celebrated Hanukkah, the festival of lights.

During the early settling of America, the celebration of Christmas was suppressed. In the 17th century, the Puritans not only banned the singing of carols, but outlawed hanging green boughs and mistletoe. They even proclaimed Christmas to be a fast day. In 1659, a law was passed in Massachusetts making the keeping of Christmas a penal offense: one could be fined five shillings for greeting a neighbor or friend with "Merry Christmas."

This atmosphere continued for over a century. As German and other European immigrants came to America in the later 1700s, however, they brought with them many of their Christmas traditions. Soon the observation of Christmas as a joyful holiday came back into popularity. In 1836, Alabama became the first state to proclaim Christmas a legal holiday; by 1890, each of the states and territories of the United States had done the same.

ADVENT WREATH

Origin

As long winter nights began in the countries of northern Europe, people would gradually stop the activities of summer and fall. Farm tools were put away, and the wheels from wagons taken off to be replaced with runners that could move over snow.

The wheels were usually stored on the walls inside the house to protect them from the elements. To remind themselves of life and hope, the people would bring in evergreen boughs and place them on the wheels. Candles were attached to the wheels to shed more light in the dark houses.

These decorated wagon wheels formed the basis for the Christian symbolism of the Advent wreath. The wreath is round, with no beginning or ending, reminding us that God is everlasting. The greens are a sign of hope and life. They come from outside where the earth is resting, and suggest the continuation of life.

The four candles represent the thousands of years people waited for the coming of the Savior, and mark each of the Sundays of Advent. The colors of the candles vary according to tradition and availability. Often, three of the candles are purple, the color of royalty and also of penance. The candle for the third week is frequently pink, a symbol of hope. It reminds us that the waiting time will soon be over. In recent years, dark blue candles have also become popular for the Advent wreath.

Connection

Advent comes at a dark and often cold time of year, a time when it is difficult to feel like a person of hope and joy. Making an Advent wreath gives us a chance to pause and let its symbols focus us on God's call. Evergreens show us constancy, no matter what outside forces bring. Candles promise warmth and a way to see clearly in darkness. The wreath reminds us that life comes around and goes around; through it all, God remains with us.

Extension

•Keep the Advent wreath present throughout the Christmas season. Replace the colored candles with white ones, and add festive ribbons, flowers, or other holiday trim to the wreath. Place a special candle in the middle of the wreath to celebrate Christ's birth.

Let family members or students take turns lighting the Advent wreath. As the candles are lit, invite each person in the group to mention someone who has been a light for them during that day.

•Make an Advent wreath within a small Christian community by inviting each person to bring one bough of evergreen, a candle, or ribbon. This activity can be a symbol of unity for the group.

•In places where candles are not allowed, such as schools, make an Advent wreath for the bulletin board. Have each person in the group trace one hand on green construction paper, and then cut it out. Encourage everyone to write on their "hand" one way they will use their hands for others during the Advent season.

Collect the paper hands, and use them to make a wreath for the bulletin board, placing the hands close to and on top of each other. Roll paper into four cones for candles, and attach these to the bulletin board wreath. Each week, attach a paper flame to a candle to help mark the time until Christmas.

•As a way to remember the people of the northern countries who took the wheels off their wagons in winter, try to take one day a week during Advent where the car remains parked; walk, if possible, to destinations.

BEES

Origin

Legend has it that bees hummed Psalm 100 to Jesus on the night of his birth. In the Middle Ages, it was thought that on Christmas the bees woke up and hummed wonderful songs of praise for Jesus, but only people who were holy enough could hear the humming.

In England, some still believe that bees buzz lullabies on Christmas Eve. Many British people honor bees by decorating their hives with holly, then going to the barnyard with wassail to offer a toast to the bees' good health. A comparable German tradition is to decorate the hives with holly so that when the bees come outside the hive they can share in the Christmas Day celebration.

Bees were said to have come from heaven; perhaps that's the reason candles made of beeswax are used in Christian worship services! Bees are a symbol of tireless activity and the industrious use of time. Besides making honey, they pollinate flowers and many important food items. Is it any wonder they have a special place in some Christmas celebrations?

Connection

At Jesus' birth, legend tells us that the bees buzzed for him. It is when our own lives settle into a monotonous buzz that we can really hear God's message. Bees also have a reputation for being in a hurry, but they slowed down to interact with Jesus. Advent is an ideal time to slow down our pace of life, open our ears to listen better, and spend more time in quiet conversation with God.

Extension

•According to aerodynamic scientists, the bumblebee should not be able to fly because its body is too heavy and its wings too frail. The bee does not know that, however, so it goes about its way in flight. Use the image of a bee as the focus for your family or classroom prayer. Ask each person to mention something which they are good at, something they do to bring happiness into their life and the lives of others.

•Using this recipe, make "Saints' Honey":

    3-4 firm, ripe pears

    1 1/4 cups sugar

    pinch nutmeg

    1/4 lemon, thinly sliced

    1/2 teaspoon ginger

    1/2 cup water

Peel, core, and chop the ripe pears into a two-quart pot. Add the remaining ingredients. Boil 12-15 minutes until the mixture looks like jam. Pour into a clear, tightly sealed jar and refrigerate. Use as soon as possible. As you eat it, think of the bees singing for Jesus.

•Include honey in several dishes to be served at home during Advent, or offer students a cracker with honey on it after class one day.

•Be like a bee and sing the praise of God in everything you do. Read Psalm 100 and think about why the bees are credited with humming it.

•Find food for thought in Proverbs 24:13–14, Proverbs 25:16, Ezekiel 20:6, Psalm 119:103.

BELLS

Origin

From ancient times, bells have been used to call people to prayer, to celebrate, to warn, to mourn. Bells were first developed in the Orient, but moved quickly into other cultures and places. Early pagan people believed that each night, evil spirits would take away the sun; each morning before dawn, the people rang bells to bring back the sun.

Bells figure prominently in the Christian tradition. To this day, bells are an important fixture in most churches, and provide the community with a sense of tradition and stability.

In many parts of the world, Christmas is announced by bells. During the Advent season, bells are used on street corners to invite people to share with the poor. Jingle bells are a popular Christmas ornament, and handbells accompany carolers in many churches and recitals.

One old story tells how when Christ was born, the devil died. To mark the devil's death, a mournful, single-toned bell would be rung for an hour before the Christmas Eve celebration. This was called the "old lad's passing bell" (the "old lad," of course, was the devil). At midnight, the bell would be changed from a mourning toll to peals of joy.

In another Christmas ritual of times past, the bell ringer would climb into the bell tower just at sunset on Christmas Eve to strike the bell with a special chiming hammer. The sound was crisp and bright, said to be like an angel's song, and could be heard for miles around. This heralded the beginning of the Christmas Eve festivities.

Bells used in liturgical celebrations at other times of the year are silenced during Lent. The Mass on Holy Thursday calls for a loud and clamorous ringing of bells during the Gloria. The bells are then silenced, until they are rung again in similarly exuberant fashion at the Gloria of the Easter Vigil Mass. In place of bells during that time, boards are clapped together, a reminder that these three days of the Triduum are a most solemn time.

Connection

Bells call us to attention. When one rings, we look away from what we are doing. A bell sends the message that something is different, something special is about to happen.

Often in our lives, things that once were special can become ordinary. Take a moment to remember the first time you did something, for example, learning to ride a bicycle, or to cook, or to fish, or play the piano, or read, or pray. What made this time special? What signaled the event? How can you again make this ordinary practice into something special once in a while?

Extension

•Remember the presence of God whenever a bell is heard. Many towns have clocks that chime the hour; clocks in the home can also be a reminder. Even wristwatches that beep at certain times can help us know we are about God's work.

•Cut bell shapes out of colored paper. Think of occasions that are announced with a bell. Write down one such event on each bell, then attach them to a tree branch or bulletin board.

•As you go about the ordinary during this time—brushing

your teeth, getting dressed, going to school or work—pause to think about what you are doing. Take special care to be aware of the actions required. Celebrate what you are doing, and remember what it was like to do this action for the first time.

•Use bells to announce the meal prayer for your Christmas dinner. Once everyone has gathered, pray this blessing:

Gracious God, we announce this gathering with the ringing of bells. May our time together be filled with celebration and joy. Thank you for the many blessings you have given us, and for the gifts that we share with one another. Give us the courage and strength to bring the Good News of Jesus to all whom we meet. Amen.

•Make bells from egg cartons. First, cut the cups of the carton apart, and decorate with paints or colored paper. Poke a hole in the bottom of each cup. Tie a ribbon through the hook of a small Christmas ball, and run this through the hole in the egg cup for a clapper. Use the finished bells for Christmas tree ornaments or decorations.

BOXING DAY

Origin

Boxing Day is celebrated on December 26 in Great Britain, Canada, and Australia. The theme for this day is giving to the needy; the name may have come from a special poor box that was placed in the church for donations on the day after Christmas.

In feudal times on this particular day, servants would carry boxes around to collect a bonus from the lord of the manor. Another English custom was to take a box aboard every vessel that sailed from port on Christmas Day. Offerings of money would be placed in it according to each sailor's ability. The box was then sealed, and not opened until the ship returned to home port. The money was removed and given to a needy person, who would show appreciation to the sailors with a special favor or service.

In current times, Boxing Day is often marked by giving a small gift of money to someone who has been of service to the family during the year, such as the mailperson or a grocer. Another practice is for people to select a favorite Christmas present, and "box" it up to give to the poor.

Connection

Boxing Day is a time to show generosity, not in return for a gift having been received, but in thoughtfulness to someone who is usually taken for granted. This generosity suggests that we give something of what we actually need, like the widow in scripture who gave a few coins and was praised by Jesus. Giving to those in need helps us imitate the generosity of God shown in the many gifts and blessings we receive.

Extension

• For each new article received at Christmas, select a used one in good condition and give it to the needy and poor. If money gifts were received for Christmas, a portion of them could be given to a food bank or another charitable organization.

• In preparation for next Christmas, decorate several small boxes for the purpose of saving money. Each box's donation can have a specific function: to help pay someone's electric bill; to buy mittens, clothing, or school supplies for children who can't afford these things; to buy a gift certificate to a restaurant for someone (or a family) who otherwise wouldn't have the money to enjoy a meal out.

Have family members or students contribute on a weekly or monthly basis during the year, then distribute the money to the designated parties during the following Christmas season.

• As part of the family gift exchange, have each person box up a new gift, or something used in good condition. Place this under the tree with all other gifts. These gifts remain unopened until Boxing Day, when they can be delivered to someone who would be surprised to receive something. (Wouldn't the person who works at a recycling place, or your doctor, or a postal worker, or store clerk be surprised to receive an unexpected gift?)

• Find food for thought in Exodus 35:5, Proverbs 11:25, and 2 Corinthians 8: 2–4.

BREADS

Origin

Bread is the staff of life. Most countries use some type of bread as a staple food, nourishing, but generally rather plain. In Christian cultures, Christmas and Easter are traditionally times when breads take on a new look. Often, sweet ingredients such as nuts, raisins, and honey are added to make the usual breads more festive, and the dough is enriched by many eggs.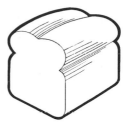

One medieval legend tells how Mary and Joseph, on their way to Egypt to escape Herod, became exhausted and stopped at a home in one of the villages. The woman of the house was busy kneading bread, and answered their knock by calling them to come in.

The Holy Family had barely gotten settled when a rough voice was heard from outside: Herod's soldiers were searching each house in the village, looking for Jesus. Joseph and Mary quickly gave the baby to the woman, and asked her to hide him. The woman promptly placed him in the pan of dough, and folded it over him so that he was hidden. She then called the soldiers to come in, while she continued to make her bread.

The soldiers looked throughout the house, but could not find the baby Jesus. When they finally left, the woman removed Jesus from the dough, and gave him back to Mary and Joseph. After that, the woman's dough rose higher and was lighter than ever before. She never ran out of dough, and was able to break off pieces of the dough to give to anyone who needed it.

Bread comes in many shapes and textures: round or long, flat or tall, croissants, pita, braided with nuts and raisins, spread as a crust for pizza. Whatever our culture or tradition, bread is an important part of our lives and of our holiday celebrations.

Connection

Bread is often taken for granted, but perhaps this is the way bread should be. It is the basis of so many meals, and the ingredients for ordinary bread are simple and plentiful. Jesus is known as the Bread of Life. He chose a very ordinary symbol to remind us of his presence among us. He chose something that is plentiful, that all people, rich and poor, would be able to have. This anonymous poem, found in a cookbook, says much about bread:

> Be gentle when you touch bread.
> Let it not be uncared for, unwanted...
> > too often bread is taken for granted.
> There is such beauty in bread:
> > beauty of sun and soil,
> > beauty of patient toil.
> Wind and rain have caressed it,
> > Christ often blest it
> Be gentle when you touch bread.

Extension

• At a family meal or before class starts, place a slice of bread on a plate and offer a special blessing, such as:

Gracious God, thank you for our daily bread. Thank you for the way you care for us and bring us to this moment. Help us to share this bread with each other and with those less fortunate than we. Amen.

Pass the bread. As each person tears off a piece they can mention one person or situation that needs to be remembered in prayer.

• Bread is mentioned in the Bible over 330 times. It is a powerful symbol throughout both the Hebrew Testament and the Christian Testament, and a central focus throughout much of the Gospel of John. Take some time to leaf through all four Gospels and notice how bread is used in just these four books.

•Read aloud with your children "The Dough and the Child," found in the book *Hark! A Christmas Sampler*, by Jane Yolen. You may also enjoy reading *Bread, Bread, Bread*, by Ann Morris. Notice the types of bread people from various countries enjoy.

•Invite several families in your parish or neighborhood to make a bread representative of their ethnic tradition. Select a date and a place for all to gather to share their bread and the stories that go with the bread.

CAMEL

Origin
During the Christmas season, camels are honored as the beasts that carried the Wise Men to visit the infant Jesus. The one-humped camel has been domesticated in the Middle East for the last 5,000 years; to this day, it still provides many people in that part of the world with transportation,

milk, meat, wool, hides, and dried manure for fuel.

The natural characteristics of camels enable them to withstand sand and wind, thus ensuring good transportation for long journeys in the desert. Since they are a main means of transportation, camels are commonly called "the ships of the desert."

One tradition of the Middle Ages held that many of the animals portrayed in the Nativity scene could actually talk like humans at midnight on Christmas Eve. However, legend also says that any person who listened to the animals was then doomed to disaster.

In Puerto Rico today, children put grass in boxes, then set the boxes on the roofs of their houses. They believe that on Christmas Eve, the Magi jump from roof to roof and replace the grass with gifts.

Connection
Camels do not have practical value to people of Western cultures,

yet they are very important to the people of the Middle East. What do you value as a necessity that other people don't even have or can't afford? Advent is a time of waiting and watching, a chance to review what are the true necessities of life and what are superfluous. Perhaps we may be holding onto possessions that we no longer need; but we might also be holding onto grudges, or bad memories. Letting go of what hinders us spiritually will allow us to grow in Christian faith and love.

Extension

• Place a camel at a distance from your Nativity scene, and each day move it closer to the stable.

• Have a camel day during Advent. During all or part of that day, give praise to God in your work or play. Think about what it means to praise God through activity. Be aware of each action or thought that is part of this day.

• As a choral reading, recite the poem "We Three Camels" from *Hark! A Christmas Sampler* by Jane Yolen. Then read the Syrian legend, "The Littlest Camel," as adapted in *Hark! A Christmas Sampler*.

• Find food for thought in Isaiah 60:6 and Judges 5:6.

CANDLES

Origin

Candles or oil lamps have long been a source of light, a way to push back the darkness. Candles are used to celebrate major life events, yet they also bring warmth and light to ordinary family meals or prayer services.

From early in Christianity the candle has been a symbol of Christ. A candle is lit when a person is baptized, then sent home to be used as a reminder that Christ lives within each person. The Easter vigil focuses on the Paschal candle, as it is brought into an unlit church, dispelling darkness in its path.

In some parts of the world, candles are lighted on Christmas as a symbol of cheerfulness and good luck. The Irish light a specially decorated candle on Christmas Eve, then pray for the people who are important to them. They are also credited with placing candles in their windows on Christmas, to provide a guiding light for any strangers seeking shelter.

Polish people often put blessed candles in the center of their tables, sometimes placed in a loaf of bread rather than in a candlestick. This combines the symbolism of Jesus as the "bread of life" and the "light of the world" in a beautiful and touching way.

Connection

Candles remind us of Jesus, the light of the world. Jesus came to push away the darkness. He told us all to not hide, but to let our light shine out. Darkness can often be found on the most bright, sunny day, in the hearts of people who are closed to love and life. As bearers of the light of Christ, we should try, at least once a day, to brighten another's path through listening and caring.

Extension

•Place a candle in the middle of the family meal table, or in a prominent place during class. Light the candle to symbolize our unity in Christ. Reflect for a few moments on the importance of light in our lives.

•Light your child's baptismal candle each year on his or her birthday. If you are in a classroom setting, have the students bring in their baptismal candles one day. Spend some time talking about the significance of our baptism, and how we are called to be light for the world, along with Christ.

•Put electric or battery-run candles in the windows of your home during the Christmas season. Each night, when it is time to light the candles, offer a short prayer for people who are searching for shelter: *Gracious God, thank you for the gift of a home. Please guide all people who are searching for a home to safe shelter this night. Give them the strength to continue their search until they are safe and warm.*

•Try turning off some of the lights on certain nights of Advent and donate the money saved on the electric bill to a group that

provides assistance to the poor in paying their heat or electric bills.
- •Give the gift of candles to others this Christmas.
- •Find food for thought in Matthew 4:16, John 1:4–5, John 8:12.

CHRISMONS

Origin

The word "chrismon" is a combination of two words: Christ and monogram. Chrismons are symbols that represent Christ, and can be made out of felt, styrofoam, wood, paper, yarn, beading, and even metal. Since there is little historical information on chrismons, we can assume that this tradition is of relatively recent origin.

Some of the symbols that can be used are:

crown - Christ the King

manger - Jesus' birthplace

sun - Jesus, the daystar

cross - Jesus died on a cross

fish - symbol of Christ

shepherd's staff - Jesus, the Good Shepherd

chi rho - Greek symbol for Christ

Traditionally, chrismons were white, a symbol of the purity of Christ, and gold, representing Christ's kingship. More recently, chrismons were decorated with jewels and pieces of lace, rickrack, and other sewing notions. Often chrismons are placed on a Jesse tree during Advent.

Connection

Jesus shows us the way, and is present in all of life. As we take time to reflect on the various symbols of Jesus, think of qualities of Jesus that bring hope and joy to others. During the Christmas season find ways to share that hope and joy.

Extension

• Families can create placemats with a few chrismon symbols on them. These placemats can then be used for family meals during Advent and Christmas.

• Arrange for your students, or a few families, to visit a nursing home for an hour or so. There, seniors and visitors can create a few chrismons, which can then be used to decorate the rooms of the nursing home, or brought back to share with the parish.

• Encourage creativity by inviting the members of your parish to design different symbols for Jesus. Hang the symbols on the wall of a prominent parish area during the Christmas season. A card explaining the meaning of each symbol could be attached.

• Use chrismons for gift package decorations. Make them with a string and attach them in such a way that they can be removed from the package and attached to the tree.

CHRISTMAS CAROLS

Origin

The word "carol" actually comes from a Greek word which describes a ring dance with flutes for accompaniment. Originally, carols were sung as people held hands and danced in a circle.

The first Christmas hymns were mentioned in fifth-century writings. Most likely, the texts were psalms from the Bible, although this custom was not widespread. Italy seems to have been the first country to have Christmas carols similar to what we now know. Tunes from secular songs were made into parodies with a Christian message. Eventually, this practice became so popular that the church made carols part of its celebration of Christmas.

Mummers were groups in the Middle Ages who went from house to house performing plays and singing, particularly at Christmas. They had a large repertoire of Christmas songs, and likely set the precedent for caroling through the streets.

Today, carols are popular throughout the Christian world. In Naples, residents play songs on their bagpipes as they march through the neighborhood. Swedish families gather to sing as they join hands in dance around the Christmas tree. In Austria, bell ringers go from house to house singing and are rewarded with the cookies that hang on the Christmas tree. The Welsh give a prize to the writer of the best new carol of the year. On Christmas Eve, Chinese Christians dress in elaborate costumes, carry lanterns, and sing Christmas carols as they parade up and down the street.

Connection

Singing is an important part of the Christmas celebration. How much fun it is to join with others to sing at Christmas, whether at home or at church! It has been said that whoever sings, prays twice. As we listen to the words of our favorite Christmas carols this year, let us reflect on what they mean in our lives today. Perhaps Christmas carols tell us a bit about God's love for us, and our relationship to others.

Extension

•Prepare a song or dance to present to the family, or in class, as part of your Christmas festivities.

•Select a favorite Christmas carol for each week during Advent. Make it a part of morning prayer in your house, or use it to open your weekly lesson.

•Make a chain of construction paper rings. On each ring, write the names of a special person who "sings" of God's love for the world.

•Use the melody of a traditional carol and make up new words to tell the story of your family, and how they like to celebrate Christmas.

•Ask a friend or family member to tell you their favorite carol. Make or buy a cassette tape with this song on it, and give it to them as a Christmas present.

• Find food for thought in Ephesians 5:19, Colossians 3:17, and James 5:13.

CHRISTMAS COOKIES

Origin

Baking cookies is one of the most popular and common of all Christmas traditions. It is a ritual that is handed down through the generations, and forms the basis for many warm and happy childhood memories.

As with breads, many countries have cookies that are special to Christmas time. In Germany, cookies filled with honey, nuts, and spices called *pfeffernüsse* have been made for hundreds of years. The Germans are also known for their gingerbread people which are baked and hung on the Christmas tree, and used as treats for guests. The children of Belgium often find a piece of angel cake under their pillows on Christmas. In Holland, people make Dutch letters and fill them with almond paste.

The English make cookies filled with mincemeat. These are rectangular in shape to symbolize the manger, and are filled with spices from the east, a reminder of the gifts of the Wise Men. English custom holds that eating some mincemeat during the twelve days of Christmas brings good luck, and so during this time mincemeat cookies are left on the table for family and guests to nibble at.

Connection

Cookies are used for after school snacks, for parties and receptions, and to provide quick energy during the day. It takes many special ingredients to make cookies. They can be as simple as a sugar cookie or as complicated as a gingerbread person. Cookies are baked with care by children and adults, and are a favorite treat for both, as well.

Our God looks after this world with tenderness and care, and graces us with special sweetness at many moments in our lives. We are reminded of this particularly during the Christmas season, as we encounter the joy and peace of this festive time.

Extension

•Make gingerbread cookies. Before they are baked make a hole in the top with a toothpick or straw so that they can be hung on the tree and offered as treats for visitors.

•Put together a cookbook of favorite cookie recipes. This cookbook can then be copied and shared with relatives and friends. If known, write a brief history of why each cookie is special to your family.

•As a group, choose a special cookie recipe, and then invite each person to bring one of the ingredients to the next gathering. Place the ingredients in a sack and attach the cookie recipe. Give the bag to someone who is special to the group.

•Prepare plates of Christmas cookies to share with others. Before they are taken to be shared, pray a blessing such as:

Gracious God, bless the friends with whom we share these cookies. May they be blessed with joy, peace, and hope. Thank you for giving us the ability to make and share them with others. Amen.

•Decorate sugar cookies to give to shut-ins or nursing home residents. Make the cookies ahead of time and have cake decorating materials available for the children to use. Place a few cookies in small plastic bags, then tie with a colorful ribbon.

•Hold a bake sale of Christmas cookies. Donate the money raised to a food pantry or homeless shelter.

CHRISTMAS TREE

Origin

In pre-Christian times, trees were often brought inside the house during winter to reassure the family that there was life through death. Many early Christians took flowering trees, such as hawthorn or cherry, into the house so they could bloom and bring fruit on Christmas Eve.

Legends abound about the Christmas tree. One story places its origin in the garden of Eden. It is said that Adam took either an apple or a sprout from the tree of knowledge; from this tree, many years later, came the wood for the cross on which Jesus died. Another similar legend has it that in the garden of Eden, the fir tree had both flowers and fruits, until Eve took off one of the fruits. From that time on it grew only needles, blossoming one time more on the eve of the Nativity.

A German legend tells of a woodsman and his family. As they were preparing for bed one night, they heard a knock on the door. There stood a child, shivering, with a look of hunger. The family took the child in, giving him food and a place to sleep. In the morning, a choir of angels sang out above the house; they then understood that it was the child Jesus whom they had cared for. Before Jesus left the family, he took a twig from a fir tree, and stuck it in the ground. This was the gift of the evergreen tree, which always bears fruit at Christmas.

Christmas trees became part of European culture during the 17th century. Fir trees decorated with paper roses, apples, sugar, gold, and wafers were popular first with royalty, then nobility, and finally with the common people. The Germans are credited with bringing the custom of the Christmas tree to America when they came to help the English fight the colonists in the mid-18th century.

Many countries have special traditions surrounding the Christmas tree. In Denmark, the Christmas tree is secretly decorated by the parents and hidden from the children until Christmas Eve. Then the tree is lighted, and the family dances around it singing favorite hymns. Philippine families decorate their entire homes with flags, palms, and colorful flowers, rather than bring a tree indoors. Chinese people call Christmas trees the "tree of light," and cover them with paper flowers, paper chains, and cotton snowflakes. To the Scottish, cutting down an entire tree is wasteful, so they make a triangular wooden frame and put evergreens on it to represent a tree.

Connection

The Christmas tree can be seen to represent Christ, the light of the world and the tree of life. A tree was critical to the story of Adam and Eve, and figured in the death of Jesus on a wooden cross. We can reflect on the universality of the Christmas tree today, and see how this symbol of our Christian heritage unites us in the celebration of Jesus' birth. The evergreen color represents the hope that Jesus brings, while the triangular shape of the tree reminds us of the mystery of the Trinity.

Extension

• Use small fir tree seedlings as gifts for Christmas visitors, or to give to students in class. These can then be kept at home, as a reminder throughout winter of the new life brought in spring, and of the new life given through the birth of Jesus.

• Bless your family or classroom Christmas tree with the following prayer: *Jesus, this tree reminds us that you are the tree of life and the light of the world. Bless this tree we have decorated to honor and celebrate your birthday. Help us remember that Christmas is a time of love and joy. Let this tree remind us to share your love with others, especially those who may not feel joy at this time. Amen.*

• Have a small real or artificial tree in each person's bedroom and let each decorate it with their personal treasures.

• Keep two sturdy branches from your Christmas tree, or cut the trunk in two after taking off the branches from the tree. Store and dry the wood until Lent, then place it in the shape of a cross to be used as part of your lenten practice.

• Read aloud "The Fir Tree," from *Hark! A Christmas Sampler* by Jane Yolen.

•Pray the "Blessing Prayer for the Planting of a Tree" from *Prayers for the Domestic Church* by Edward Hays.

COWS

Origin

According to Nativity stories, cows are said to have used their breath to warm the infant Jesus as he lay in the manger. Some farm families in England take a wassail bowl into the barnyard on Christmas Eve, and drink a toast to the health of the animals, while some Polish farm families serve unleavened bread to their horses and cows at Christmas time. A Norwegian custom is to give the cow an extra meal on Christmas Eve.

According to a tradition of the Middle Ages, the cow was one of the animals that could talk like humans at midnight on Christmas Eve. But no human could listen to the animals talking, for it would bring bad luck if they did. German legend, however, holds that a person born between eleven and twelve o'clock on Christmas Eve could understand what the cattle were saying without bad luck happening to them.

Connection

It is easy to take cows and other animals for granted; we forget that they supply milk and meat so that we can grow strong and healthy. Yet we often take those we love most for granted as well, and forget to thank them for both little and big things. Not only should we thank them with words, but perhaps do something to show our appreciation. During Advent, let us thank God for all of the people we sometimes take for granted, and think of all the people who do things that effect our lives in a positive way.

Extension

•As a family or class, send a note of appreciation to someone in public office. These people are often taken for granted.

•Have a toast with milk to our God who created cows who provide milk for nurturing our physical self. The toast may be something like this: *We honor you, God, for making cows that give us milk to make us healthy for doing your work.*

•The cow has great importance for providing us with meat and milk from which many other products are made. Figure out how much it costs for the milk and meat you eat each day or week and donate that amount to a food bank.

•As choral reading with your family or class, recite the poem "The Praising Cows," from *Hark! A Christmas Sampler* by Jane Yolen.

•Find food for thought in Isaiah 11:7.

CRACKERS & NOISEMAKERS

Origin

Crackers, also known as "poppers," are brightly colored oblong tubes filled with candy and gifts. When the ends are pulled, there is a loud bang, and the contents of the cracker spill onto the table. This custom is popular in England, but the people of France use a similar table favor.

Crackers may have been developed to bring the noisemakers and fireworks that were popular in other countries into the house. On Christmas Eve, the people of China, France, and other countries use firecrackers to announce Midnight Mass. The people of Ceylon use drums and firecrackers on Christmas Eve to keep the evil spirits away, and in Africa, fireworks are considered part of the Christmas day festivities.

Noisemakers are used in Easter celebrations as well. In Mexico and South American countries, there is a custom called "burning Judas." A small Judas figure is made from rags, paper, or straw, and firecrackers are stuffed inside. When the church bells ring out for the Easter vigil, new fires are lit and the Judas figures are burned.

Connection

Noise is often disruptive of our regular routine. The truck backing up makes a lot of noise. The screaming of the emergency vehicles calls us to pause and step out of the way or pull to the side. During the busy holiday preparations, take time, when noise interrupts your routine, to think of the gift of noise and how it calls us to a different way of being.

Extension

•In your family, class, or group, make crackers for a meal or other occasion. You will need:

Paper tubes, about 5 inches long

Small pieces of candy and/or small gifts

Wrapping paper big enough to wrap the tube

Ribbon or yarn to fasten the paper around the tube

Fill each tube with candy and small gifts. (Or, you can put a piece of paper with a Scripture verse or wish for the new year inside.) Wrap each tube with a piece of wrapping paper, about four inches longer on each end than the tube. Tie the paper close to the tube, then fringe the ends by cutting little strips and close with the ties.

•Place a piece of a small Nativity set in the middle of a cloth napkin. Fold the napkin into a a triangular shape, then fold the bottom points up to meet the top point. Fold vertically in half. Put a folded napkin at each person's dinner plate. As the napkins are opened to begin dinner, have everyone place their Nativity piece in a crèche, or on a cake that will be eaten for dessert. The Christmas story can then be read.

•Use noisemakers to awaken family members during the Advent and Christmas season.

• As a family, choose a meal during which all members would whisper in contrast to the usual din of conversation. Note how a lowered noise level changes the interaction of the group. You can also try this in your classroom.

DONKEY

Origin

Although the donkey is not mentioned in the biblical account of Jesus' birth, tradition and custom give it a central role in the Nativity story. Because donkeys were used as beasts of burden during that time in history, it is possible that Mary and Joseph used one for transportation.

This is one of the many stories told about donkeys at the birth of Jesus: because they could find no empty rooms in Bethlehem, an innkeeper offered Mary and Joseph shelter in an adjoining stable. Leading them there, the innkeeper's wife warned Mary and Joseph to watch out for Assa, a mean little donkey who shared the stable with a cow. Assa had been treated badly by his previous owner, who beat the donkey often, and made him carry heavy loads. Consequently, the little donkey did not like people very much, and would bite and kick anyone who got in his way.

Mary, however, had a gentle face, and she smiled at the donkey as she and Joseph came into the stable. Rarely had anyone smiled at Assa! Then Joseph went to get fresh hay to prepare a bed on which the baby could lay after he was born, and he gave some of the hay to Assa and the cow to eat. This was all a bit too much for Assa to understand.

For a while, the donkey was content with this good fortune, but as the night went on, he became restless for more attention. Jesus had just been born, and Mary and Joseph were so busy with the baby that they ignored the animals entirely.

Suddenly, Assa gave a bray so loud that the baby awoke, while Joseph and Mary jumped at the sound. The donkey expected a beating for causing a commotion, but the mother only smiled and quietly said, "Hush, dear donkey. The baby must sleep. "

Assa had never experienced such kindness; for hours, he made not a sound. Later in the evening, however, the donkey was feeling hungry and noticed that some of the nicest hay had been used for the baby's bed. So Assa stuck his head under the bed and began to nibble. Suddenly, the baby woke and reached out to touch the donkey's ear. The baby smiled, and all of the pain the donkey had suffered from mean owners seemed to vanish.

When Mary awoke, she noticed that the donkey was resting quietly by the manger, while Jesus held its soft ear.

Connection

Donkeys are often the brunt of jokes. During this season, try to be aware that Jesus used donkeys as a means of transportation. Certainly, an animal that has been used in such a way deserves to be kindly treated. Are there people in our lives that are treated poorly by others? Reflect on the story above, and try to treat others with kindness, especially during the busy season of Advent and Christmas.

Extension

•Have someone in your family or class read the story of the donkey found above. In place of Assa's name, however, have the reader put in his or her own name. Does the story fit?

• Take special care to thank people who do the difficult and uncelebrated work around you, such as the janitor, the garbage people, the postal people, people who keep the streets clean or who shovel the sidewalks.

•Say "thank you" with greater sincerity to those who help you during the Advent and Christmas season. Mention specifically what you are thankful for.

•Take time to write a thank-you note to someone whose work is ordinary and usual, but whose work would really be missed if they were not there to do it.

•Pray the "Blessing Prayer for Farm Animals," from *Prayers for the Domestic Church* by Edward Hays.

EVERGREENS

Origin

For Christians, evergreens symbolize hope and everlasting life. Roman Christians hung evergreens over the windows of their houses to hide their celebrations of prayer. In pre-Christian times, people believed that spirits lived in trees, especially fruit trees and evergreens.

One legend tells of how the evergreen provided shelter for Mary, Joseph, and baby Jesus as they escaped from Herod to Egypt. As they fled along a road in Israel, they encountered a huge pine tree with brittle branches and a half-rotten trunk. The soldiers were following close behind, so the holy family hid in the hollow trunk. As they did, the pine tree dropped its branches and covered them until Herod's troops passed. When the holy family emerged from the tree, Jesus blessed it, and gave it green branches all year long.

Connection

The evergreen is a dependable tree, green all year round. Are we dependable in our relationships with other people? Are we consistent and positive in our daily contacts with others? Can others depend on us for friendship, or for our consistent quality of work?

Advent and Christmas seasons are good times to think about our relationship to the earth. Do we respect the works of nature? Do we care for the earth, and act as its stewards rather than owners? Do we preserve rather than destroy nature?

Extension

•Take the time to notice the evergreens near your home, school, or place of work. Thank God for your existence and for that of all creation.

•Place a sprig of evergreen on or near a picture of a person who has entered eternal life. Take time to pray in a special way for that person. Place a few pieces of evergreen on their grave, if the cemetery is nearby.

- Make edible evergreen wreaths. You will need:
  - 32 large marshmallows
  - 6 tablespoons butter
  - 1/2 teaspoon vanilla
  - 1/2 teaspoon almond extract
  - 1 teaspoon green food coloring
  - 4 cups of corn flakes
  - red cinnamon candies

Melt marshmallows and butter in large double boiler over low heat. Mix in the flavorings and food coloring. Add corn flakes and stir well. Take a spoonful of the mixture, drop onto waxed paper, and form into a small wreaths. Decorate with cinnamon candies before the wreaths harden.

- Put pine fragrance on a cotton ball and set it on a light bulb. Or, use pine needles in a potpourri pot or a pot of water over heat and enjoy the fragrance. This aroma is a reminder of the everlasting life that Jesus brought.
- Recycle or reuse Christmas boxes and wrappings to save a tree.
- Find food for thought in Hosea 14:9.

GIFT GIVING

Origin

The custom of gift giving at Christmas may have evolved from the winter solstice event known as Saturnalia. This celebration was meant to call back the sun, which ancient people feared had gone away. During this time, gifts of honey, fruits, lamps, and gold coins were offered to the pagan gods, while the rich gave gifts to the poor and slaves were allowed to exchange clothing with their masters.

Many countries have their own legends and traditions surrounding the practice of gift giving. In an Italian story, Befana was visited by the Wise Men on their journey to Bethlehem. She was invited to go with them, but was too busy cleaning house to join them. Afterwards, she regretted her decision, and tried to catch up to the Wise Men, only to remain forever running after them. On January 6, she travels the world on a broom leaving gifts and candy for children, just in case one of them is the child Jesus. For children who have not been good, Befana leaves bits of coal.

A similar theme is found in the Russian story of Babushka, who refused to join the Wise Men and actually directed them *away* from Bethlehem. She, too, had second thoughts and tried to catch up. As she hurried along, she left toys and gifts for children at each house, thinking one of them might be the house where Jesus lived.

Among German children, the story of Kristkindl tells how the baby Jesus travels on a white donkey leaving "Christ bundles" made up of food, toys, clothing, and helpful gifts. Dutch parents disguise gifts for the children, and hide them in funny places, including the inside of puddings. Each gift usually comes with a rhyme attached that hints at the contents of the gift, a practice that is common in Sweden, as well.

An English tradition has children writing their wish list on a piece of paper and throwing it into the back of the fireplace. If the paper goes up the chimney without burning, the child will get what was on the list. If the paper burns, another list can be written and tossed into the fireplace.

Saint Nicholas, a bishop in Asia Minor in the fourth century, is commonly seen as the model for Santa Claus. One popular account of Nicholas's generosity tells of how he helped a poor merchant pay the dowries of his three daughters. Nicholas, undetected, threw a bag of money in the window for the first daughter, then later, a second bag of money for the second daughter. When he threw the third bag, the merchant caught him and told everyone about this generous man. Soon, all unexplained gifts became credited to Saint Nicholas.

Connection

Jesus, God's most special gift to us, came "wrapped" as a person. Is it possible that the humble wrappings of Jesus sowed the seed for modern gift giving? Since Christmas is filled with gift giving and receiving, it is a good time to be thankful for the gifts—friendship, love, caring, listening—that each of us has received from other people in our lives. It is also a time to give thanks for the talents and abilities God has given us.

Extension

•In place of a tangible gift, have empty boxes that are wrapped and decorated. Each box represents a personal trait, experience, or opportunity that each person wants to thank God for.

•In your family or class, have each person contribute some money toward buying gifts for a needy person or group of people. Give them something that you would like and appreciate as well.

•Before opening Christmas gifts, bless them with the following prayer: *Loving God, giver of all gifts, we thank you for these presents. We have chosen and wrapped each with love. Please know how much we appreciate the love and the joy each of us brings to each other. We bless each other as part of God's family, through whom we come to better love you, our God.*

•Be creative and make your own gift wrapping. You can use such things as decorated brown paper bags, comics, wallpaper scraps or samples, old sheet music, or used Christmas cards. Use non-traditional packaging such as pillow cases, decorated cans, flower pots, handkerchiefs, or Christmas fabric.

•Give a gift to someone you don't know, as St. Nicholas did.

•Find food for thought in Genesis 32:11, Ecclesiastes 5:18, and Ephesians 2:8.

GOAT

Origin

Much of the history of the goat as a Christmas symbol seems to have come from the Scandinavian countries. In Sweden, the story is told that the goat

butts naughty children, so a small figure of a goat is put out among the Christmas candles to remind children to be good. On Christmas Eve, gifts are delivered by a Swedish gnome who rides in a sleigh pulled by a goat. Children leave out carrots for the goats, along with bowls of porridge for the gnome.

Shaggy goats bring gifts for the children in Finland. In Norway, the domestic animals get an extra meal on Christmas Eve, after which the Norwegian children leave out another dish of food for the goat. If it is empty the next day, it means good luck, and if it is full of grain, it means there will be a good crop that year.

In the Hebrew testament, the goat is a common animal of sacrifice in atonement for sin. The sacrifice of goats is mentioned in Genesis as part of the covenant God offered to the chosen people. In his letter to the Hebrews, Paul describes how the sacrifice of the blood of Jesus earned redemption for all and replaced the need to sacrifice the blood of goats or bulls. Perhaps the term "scapegoat" evolved from the sacrifice Jesus made for us.

Connection

Most of us would readily give up a goat for sacrifice or for any other reason. But what are some of the things we might have a harder time sacrificing if God asked us? What are some of the things we are most attached to: the telephone, the TV, our money, our houses, the car?

Are we too attached to intangible things such as an opinion, a bias, a preference, a memory, a hurt? What do we need to let go of in order to be fully Christian? What action can we take to let go of that attachment?

Extension

•Two common expressions that somewhat degrade people are when we say they are the "butt of a joke," or that they are a "scapegoat." Think of someone you know who may have been treated badly in this way, and write a list of that person's good qualities. Let that person know, in some small way, of his or her importance to other people and to God.

•Select a favorite piece of clothing, a toy, a piece of jewelry, or a knickknack. Sacrifice using or seeing that item during Advent, or cover it with a piece of cloth. Put it in a place where it can remind you to pray in thanksgiving for the sacrifice of Jesus.

•Find food for thought in Leviticus 4:23,24,28, Leviticus 16:4–26, Luke 15:29, and Hebrews 9:12–19.

GOLDEN ROSE

Origin

There is a difference of opinion concerning the custom of the golden rose. Some texts indicate that it is observed on the third Sunday of Advent, Gaudete Sunday, while others place it on Laetare Sunday, the fourth Sunday of Lent. Both of these Sundays are days of gladness, a time to look ahead to the end of a penitential season.

The German name for the third Sunday of Advent is *Rosensonntag* or the "Sunday of the rose." Popes used to carry a golden rose in their right hand when they finished celebrating Mass on the third Sunday of Advent. It is thought that this custom may have been carried over from the ancient tradition of bearing flowers through the streets of Rome to celebrate the beginning of a new season.

The custom of sending a golden rose to someone who lived an exemplary Christian life was begun in the early 11th century. Originally, the giver would send a real rose. But in time, the gift became a beautiful piece of jewelry, a rose made from gold and decorated with jewels. By the 15th century, the single gold rose was more commonly replaced by a cluster of roses decorated with precious stones. These were then blessed by the pope, and presented to special persons, cities, or churches as a token of respect.

Connection

Giving golden roses is a symbol of appreciation for someone who has been generous with their time and talent. How often do we give honor to God through prayers of praise and thanksgiving? We are protected and cared for in so many ways that we should often lift our voices in gratitude to God.

Extension

•Purchase small, gold-colored silk roses. Attach them to a card on which you have printed the story of the golden rose, and give them to shut-ins during a visit.

•Decorate golden roses cut from felt and present them to members of the social justice committee or to the church volunteers who have been exemplary in their service to others during the year.

•Children could be encouraged to make golden roses from bread dough, felt, paper, or other materials and give them to classroom aides, catechists, crossing guards, or other people who have made their lives better during the school year.

•Together, as a family or class, sing the Christmas carol, "Lo, How a Rose E're Blooming."

HOLLY

Origin

With its fiery red berries and thorny leaves, the holly bush can resemble the burning bush of the Hebrew Testament. Because of its ability to survive throughout winter, holly became a popular decoration in ancient British and Roman homes, whose residents hoped it would give similar strength to those who lived there. The berries would be placed in windows as a sign of hospitality to the spirits.

One Christian legend tells how the holly bush was once covered with white berries, and that the crown of thorns placed on Jesus' head at the crucifixion was made from holly branches. As the story goes, when the soldiers pressed the crown into Jesus' head, the white berries turned red from his blood.

Another legend says that the cross of Christ was made from the wood of a holly tree, and the red berries represent the redeeming blood Jesus shed out of love for us.

In bygone times, some believed holly had special power against witchcraft. For this reason, single women would fasten a piece of holly to their beds to keep them from turning into witches during the night. Holly was also used in German churches as protection from lightning, and as a symbol of good luck for men.

Connection

The legend of holly branches used both for the crown of thorns and for Jesus' cross connects us to the passion and death of Jesus. Yet we also use holly to decorate at Christmas, a time of joy. There are some people in our lives who give us cause for both joy and pain. Because of our love for them we are willing to tolerate the pain, and thus grow within the relationship. As the holly is a sign of Jesus' life and death, so, too, it can remind us that our relationships are usually a mixture of both joy and pain.

Extension
•Holly symbolizes hospitality. During this Christmas season, invite someone to your home who has never been a guest there, and offer them some refreshment and conversation. Share with them one of the stories about holly.

•Give away sprigs of holly and wish people "God luck."

•Wear a bit of holly as a lapel pin during Advent.

•Sing the traditional English carol, "The Holly and the Ivy."

•With your family or class, dance or march to the music of "Deck the Halls."

JESSE TREE

Origin
The Jesse tree represents Jesus' family tree. The name is taken from Isaiah 11:1, in which Jesus is referred to as a shoot coming up from the stump of Jesse, the father of David.

The ornaments on the Jesse tree tell of Jesus' ancestors, and of the events leading to Jesus' birth. While it is hard to establish when and where the custom of the Jesse tree began, it most likely started in the Middle Ages as a way to teach Bible stories.

In recent years, the Jesse tree has regained popularity as an Advent activity for both home and classroom. Some of the scripture stories and symbols frequently used on the tree are:

Adam and Eve (Genesis 3:1–7)	apple
Noah (Genesis 6:13–22)	ark or rainbow
Abraham (Genesis 12:1–12)	knife
Isaac (Genesis 22:1–19)	ram
Sarah (Genesis 12:1—13:18)	tent
Joseph (Genesis 37:12–28)	colorful coat
Moses (Exodus 34:28)	Ten Commandments

David (1 Samuel 16:17–23)	harp
Jacob (Genesis 28:10–22)	a ladder
Rachel and Leah (Genesis 29:15–30)	a veil
Miriam (Exodus 15:20–21)	tambourine
Solomon (1 Kings 3:4–15)	crown
Ruth (Book of Ruth)	anchor (for faithfulness)
Isaiah (Isaiah 11:1–9)	lion and lamb
Deborah (Judges 4)	tent peg and mallet
Joshua (Joshua 6:1–15)	trumpet
Daniel (Daniel 6:17–24)	lion
Rebecca (Genesis 25:19–34; 27)	a well
Manna (Exodus 16:4–5)	basket of bread
Elizabeth (Luke 1:39–55)	small home
Mary (Luke 1:26–38)	lily
Joseph (Matthew 1:18–25)	hammer or saw
Jesus (Luke 2:1–20)	chi–rho

Connection

Roots are important parts of a tree. As people, we need to know our roots, as well. Often, we run from one thing to another without reflecting on where we have been or where we are going. As we create a Jesse tree during this Advent season, let us pause and look at our lives to see on whose shoulders we stand.

Extension

•Make a Jesse tree for your home or classroom. First, take a large, bare branch and secure it in a pot of sand or rocks. (You can also use a large potted plant or evergreen.) Create ornaments that trace Jesus' royal line by making symbols for some of the people found in the Hebrew testament. Make the ornaments out of cardboard or construction paper, and decorate as you like. Run a string through the top of the ornament for hanging on the tree.

Instead of hanging all the ornaments on the tree at one time, you may want to hang one on every other day or so of Advent. Read the scripture citation given here as you hang each ornament on the tree. If you are making a Jesse tree for your class, have each of the students put an ornament on the tree during your Advent classtimes. (Instead of a tree, you can also make a mobile out of the Jesse symbols for your home or classroom.)

•Make a genealogical tree for your own family. Invite older relatives to share their knowledge with you to fill out the family history. Discuss people who are important to the family and create symbols to represent them. Each day, one symbol could be taken off and that person prayed for by the family. If the person is still living, call or write to let them know what your family is doing.

•A parish can make a "parish tree" or other similar listing of people who have been important to the church family, such as pastors, pastoral associates, lay ministers, catechists, teachers, janitors, parishioners, and the like. Place these people's names in a prominent place at the beginning of Advent, and invite the parish to stop by, read the "tree," and offer prayers for those listed on it.

•Some families in the area may be recent immigrants, and may miss their families and homelands. Invite them to share stories and pictures of their ancestors at a parish gathering, or in your home.

KRISTKINDL

Origin
The word Kristkindl means "Christ child" in German. This custom began as a way to prepare for the coming of Jesus by seeing him in others. The practice would start with a family, neighborhood, or other group of people. Each member would write their name on a piece of paper, then put that piece of paper into a container. Everyone would then draw a name other than their own.

Several times during the Advent season, each person would try to do something for their Kristkindls; the trick, however, was to do something without the other person finding out who did it for them. The "something special" could be a kindness, a sacrifice, or a prayer offered for the other. Each week, an anonymous note would be written to the Kristkindl telling him or her what had been done for them that week. On Christmas day, everyone would reveal his or her identity to their Kristkindl.

When this custom was brought to North America, the name was changed to "Kris Kringle."

Connection

Secrets surround the Advent and Christmas season. Certainly, the Kristkindl custom requires lots of secrets, finding ways to do something special for someone without them finding out who did it. Yet doing something special for others should be more than just a secret and seasonal event. Take a few moments to reflect on the ways we treat each other. Sometimes the person that needs to be treated with more care and appreciation is ourself.

Extension

•Place the names of family or extended family in a basket. Invite each person to draw a name. Talk about things that could be done for each other which do not require money. At the end of the season, each person could make a card for his or her secret Kris Kringle.

•In your parish or school, connect the younger students to the older students by having the older students draw the name of a younger one at the beginning of Advent. The pairs could then meet each other at a special prayer service at the beginning of Advent.

Each person could tell something special about themselves to the other. During Advent, they could meet to pray with each other. At the end of Advent each person could bring a special treat for their Kris Kringle and share it at a prayer service and Christmas party.

•Place the names of shut-ins or residents of nursing homes in a basket. Invite people from the parish to draw a name of one of them. During Advent, the parishioner could visit the shut-in or resident, make special gifts, write cards, or do some errands that would make that person's life easier.

•List various organizations that need help during Advent, such as homeless shelters or food banks. Attach the names of these groups to a tree and invite various church organizations to choose one of these groups as their Kris Kringle. The group can then call the chosen organization to see what its needs are and find ways to help.

•Go out of your way to do something kind for someone to whom you have difficulty relating.

MAGI

Origin
The name magi comes from the Greek word *mágos*, meaning "great" or "illustrious." Magi were a higher class of people who may have been members of the king's court, or doctors, scientists, astrologers, and mathematicians.

There is a tradition in the Orient that twelve Magi visited Jesus at his birth, but because of the scriptural record of three gifts (Matthew 2:11), three Magi are generally accepted. Great details about their characteristics are presented in a legend, which says that the first of the Magi to visit Jesus was called Melchior. He was believed to be the ruler of Nubia and Arabia, a man of some sixty years who brought gold to Jesus, the king.

The second of the Magi was Kaspar, ruler of Tarsus in Turkey, said to be about twenty years and beardless. He offered frankincense, symbolizing the divinity of Jesus. The third, Balthasar, ruler of Ethiopia, was forty years old and of dark complexion. He brought myrrh, which predicted the death of Jesus. (In actuality, frankincense was used for embalming, while myrrh was used as a perfume and a medicine.)

This legend further holds that Mary gave each of the Magi a linen band from the cloth in which the infant Jesus was wrapped and a small box in which there was a stone, a symbol of their solid faith. The Magi also received a special gift in return for those they had brought: charity and spiritual wealth for the gold, perfect faith for the frankincense, and truth and meekness for the myrrh.

Connection

Whether the Magi were kings, astrologers, or mathematicians, they can surely be thought of as great and illustrious people. The Magi followed a simple sign that looked like a star; although there were many stars in the sky on the night of Jesus' birth, they knew that one alone was different. Because of their answer to God's invitation, they were among the first to see the Messiah.

The story of the Magi reminds us to be sensitive to the signs God gives us through ordinary people and events. What are the signs God is giving to us? What simple actions can we do that might bring great rewards to others? How great it is to recognize God's message when we see it, and how illustrious to respond.

Extension

•The three kings' cake is a European tradition. The cake is flat, more like a cookie, and has one or two almonds, a dime, or some other tiny "prize" in it. The one to find the prize will have good fortune throughout the year. Here is the recipe for three kings' cake:

1/2 cup blanched almonds
1 cup sugar
6 tablespoons soft butter
6 teaspoons vanilla or almond extract
2 eggs, lightly beaten
2 1/4 cups flour
1 1/2 teaspoons baking powder
2 tablespoons raisins or currants

Grind the almonds with 1/4 cup sugar in a food processor or blender, then set aside. Use a fork to mix the butter and remaining sugar together in a bowl until thoroughly blended. Beat in the eggs and the extract, saving a tablespoon of egg to glaze the top.

Stir the flour and baking powder into the egg mixture. Stir in the sugar and almond mix, along with the raisins or currants, then add one or two whole almonds, a dime, or whatever other item you will use for a "prize."

Put the dough onto a greased cookie sheet. Pat the dough flat into a 1/2 inch circle. Spread the reserved beaten egg on the top of the cake. Bake at 350° for 20 minutes. Serves 12.

•On January 6th, the feast of the Epiphany, bless your house and each room with a special prayer. Use chalk and write the initials of the three kings and the current year over the entrance to your house, e.g., 19 + C + M + B + 97. The writing can stay throughout the year to remind everyone of your hospitality, and to bring blessings to those who share your home with you.

•Read the book *The Legend of Old Befana* by Tomie de Paola.

•Sing the carol "We Three Kings" as if you were among the three kings.

•Find food for thought in 1 Timothy 2:2.

MANGER/CRÈCHE

Origin

In the 13th century, Francis of Assisi originated the practice of depicting the Nativity scene as a three-dimensional setting. Prior to that time, there were paintings of the Nativity known from as far back as the year 380 CE. Francis's manger scene used live animals, people, and a wax Jesus figure. Today, although live manger recreations can be found in some churches and shrines, most manger scenes use statues to depict the Nativity scene.

The French make small clay figures for their crèche, called *santons* or "little saints." The *santons* might represent biblical characters or people from everyday life, such as a teacher or family member. In Italy, the manger scene is called a *presepio,* and serves as the center of family Christmas ceremonies. Sometimes groups of children carry their *presepios* through the streets.

It is a Bolivian custom to add something new each day to the manger, which they call *nacimiento*. Some of their figures may be only half an inch high. German manger decorations can include waterfalls, landscaping, gardens, houses, fences, and many figures. A Moravian custom is to build elaborate scenes, as large as a room, filled with recreations of small towns, rural residences, and figures from everyday life.

Connection

In any culture, it is the heart and the spirit that must prepare to receive the newness of Jesus. Advent gives us a chance to clean our spiritual house, and eliminate the excesses and ugliness so that we can be clean and open to God's Word. What needs to be removed or redecorated in our hearts and lives so Jesus can be welcome as our spiritual partner? The manger is where Jesus was born, and we are the mangers where he lives.

Extension

• As a family or class, set up a manger scene together. Talk about each figure and its significance to the Nativity. Leave the crib empty until Christmas Eve (or your last class before Christmas). Place the manger in a prominent place in your home or classroom.

Or, set up the outside of the manger on the first Sunday of Advent, and put one figure into the manger every other day or so, until Christmas. You can also place all the figures at a distance from the manger, moving them a little closer each day until they are all in place on Christmas Eve.

• Pray a blessing over your manger, such as the following:
Dearest Jesus, bless this crib that we have prepared in honor of your birth as a human being. During these next days, we will prepare a place for you in our hearts. Help each of us to make this a special time of waiting and wondering as we go about our plans to celebrate Christmas.

• Have a class or family discussion about each of the characters in the crèche. Talk about the role that each character played in the Nativity, how they may have felt, and where they fit in the overall picture. If Jesus was born today, who might be in the Nativity scene, and why?

•Your family or class may want to make their own manger scene. You can fashion figures for a crèche by using clay made from this recipe:

2 cups baking soda

1 cup cornstarch

1 1/2 cups water

Mix the baking soda and cornstarch in a saucepan. Slowly stir in 1 to 1 1/2 cups of cold water until the mixture is smooth. Cook over moderate heat, stirring constantly to avoid burning, until the mixture is stiff. Put onto a cookie sheet and cool.

When the dough is cool, knead it until pliable. Tint some of the dough with food coloring by putting the coloring in the middle of a small amount of the clay, then blending it in. Shape the figures in the Nativity scene, using a picture from a Christmas book as a guide. If you want to save any leftover dough, store each color in a separate container or plastic bag.

•To make a manger, cut an oatmeal or salt box in half lengthwise. Cover the outside with brown construction paper or a grocery bag, then arrange your clay figures inside and around the manger.

•A piece of straw or yarn may be placed in the manger each day to symbolically prepare a soft place for baby Jesus to be laid. Each piece can represent a good deed, a kind word, or a special prayer. Make a brief classroom ritual, or a family mealtime or bedtime ritual, out of placing the straw in the manger.

•Cut strips of yellow paper, and place in a bowl by the manger in your home or classroom. Each day before the family meal (or before each class), have everyone gathered take a piece of paper. Then, have everyone write down one kind action they have observed during the day. Put the piece of paper into the manger.

•Pray the "Blessing Prayer for the Christmas Crib" from *Prayers for the Domestic Church* by Edward Hays.

•Sing "The Stable Hymn," found in *Hark! A Christmas Sampler* by Jane Yolen.

•Read the book *The Last Straw,* by Paula Palangi.

MISTLETOE

Origin

The ancient Druids considered mistletoe a sacred plant because it grows with its roots wrapped around a tree, and not in the ground. As part of the winter solstice celebration on December 21, a Druid priest would climb an oak tree and and cut down the mistletoe. People stood under the tree and caught the plant in their clothing, so that the mistletoe would not fall on the ground and bring bad luck.

Norse men and women also thought of mistletoe as sacred, and believed that it had the power to make poisons harmless, humans and animals fertile, and protect people from witchcraft and evil spirits while bringing good luck and blessings. This belief grew out of a story about a goddess of love, whose son was killed by an arrow made from mistletoe. When the goddess cried, her tears fell on the mistletoe and turned into white berries. She promised that the mistletoe would never harm anyone again; rather, anyone who would stand under the mistletoe would receive a kiss.

This custom originally became a means to announce a couple's engagement, and was seen as a pledge of love and an omen of happiness, good fortune, fertility, and long life. A further practice evolved from this custom, that any enemies who met under the mistletoe, whether accidentally or deliberately, must put down their weapons and declare a truce for the day. This carried over to homes, where families would hang a sprig over the doorway as a pledge of peace and friendship.

During the 17th century, the English forbade hanging mistletoe in their attempt to stifle the celebration of Christmas. After this prohibition was relaxed, mistletoe became a symbol of Christ, the divine healer, and was distributed throughout churches with a holy wish for pardon and redemption.

Although mistletoe is seldom used in church decorations today because of its pagan connection, the traditions of healing, peace, friendship, and love associated with mistletoe make it an apt Christmas symbol.

Connection

With its reputation as a healing plant, mistletoe reminds us that Jesus is our healer if we let him be. Let us pray about the wounds in the world that need healing, then reflect on ways we can go about bringing Jesus, the healer, to these situations. Perhaps we need to share in the healing of those who kill by polluting the air and water, or by destroying trees, or by repeating rumors, or by favoring human destruction, or by promoting public policies that harm creation. Take action with a letter, phone call, or personal contact.

Extension

• The apostle Paul, in his many letters, often tells the readers to "greet one another with the holy kiss." Give a holy kiss to someone by telling them "I love you" for the first time.

• Phone or write to someone with whom you had been friends, but have lost contact.

• Take a piece of mistletoe and put it in a clear container. Before a meal or snack, pass the container around the table, offering a wish of peace as it is handed over.

• Give a piece of mistletoe to someone with whom you have had a quarrel, as a sign of love and healing.

• Find food for thought in Luke 7:38, Proverbs 24:26, and 2 Corinthians 13:12.

OJO DE DIOS

Origin

The ojo de Dios, or "eye of God," is a woven, diamond-shaped hanging that originated among Mexican Indian tribes. Today, it is used as a Christmas decoration, and carries a wish for long life, good fortune, and good health. The shape of the ojo de Dios is reminiscent of both a star and of a cross, and its name may have come from the passage in Psalm 33 which reads "the eyes of the Lord are on the righteous."

Connection

We make an ojo de Dios from everyday materials, two sticks and some yarn wound together, which then become something beautiful. How often do we overlook the beauty in common, everyday things: the beauty of nature, of people, of personal relationships, the shape of a tree, the intricacy of our highway system, the variety of food products available to us, and the presence of electricity? The ojo de Dios reminds us to enjoy the beauty of the common, usual experiences and events of our lives.

Extension

• Make and give an ojo de Dios to those through whose behavior you see God. You will need:

2 sticks or twigs of the same length

various colors of yarn

glue and scissors

Tie the sticks or twigs with yarn to form a cross. Using the same ball of yarn, begin wrapping one arm of the ojo de Dios by going under and around, then moving counterclockwise, wrap the next arm under and around. Continue wrapping in this manner, keeping the yarn taut and the sticks at right angles.

To start a new color, tie it to the previous color and try to have the knot on one of the arms. When finished, tie the yarn to one of the arms. For a variation, part of the wrapping could be done over and around, moving the ojo in a clockwise direction.

• Look out the window and thank God for the clouds, the blades of grass, the breeze, flowers, trees, or whatever catches your eye.

• The ojo de Dios should symbolize an important characteristic of the maker. Design and make an ojo de Dios that represents you, your group, or your family.

• Do something for someone who is blind or partially sighted. If you don't know someone with limited vision, visit a nursing home and offer to read to one of the sight-impaired residents. You might also volunteer to read on tape for distribution among the blind.

• Find food for thought in Psalm 33:18.

OPLATEK

Origin

This Polish custom symbolizing forgiveness and unity dates back to pre-Christian times, and is still practiced in many Polish homes throughout the world. The word "oplatek" is thought to be from the Latin *oblatum*, meaning "holy bread."

The oplatek, or Christmas wafer, is unleavened bread; perhaps this is a reference to manna, the unleavened bread given to the Hebrews as they wandered in the desert (Exodus 16:31). The oplatek is embossed with a picture of the Nativity scene or other Christmas-related picture. Often, the wafer is obtained before the first Sunday of Advent and then displayed on the family table during the Advent season. In some homes, straw is placed under the tablecloth and then the Christmas wafer placed on top.

Before the Christmas vigil meal, each person at the table is given a piece of the oplatek. They then take their piece around to each member of the family, breaking off a bit of each other's bread while sharing a brief expression of love. If there is a wrong from the past year between two people, this is the time to mend the rift by asking for forgiveness and reconciliation.

This custom can also be observed by giving the wafer to the eldest person at the table, who breaks off a piece, and then passes it on to the next person at the table, who then does the same. After the eldest family member offers a blessing for health, happiness, and forgiveness, the pieces of oplatek are eaten and the family sits down to share the meal.

To include those who were not present for the Christmas vigil meal, pieces of the oplatek were sent to them in letters. Sometimes, wafers would be given to the animals on Christmas Eve in petition for their good health.

This wonderful custom provides people with a way to celebrate forgiveness for the wrongs that have occurred during the past year, and to celebrate the hope that much good will be in store in the coming year for all who sit at the table.

Connection

One of the saddest situations in any family is when one member has not spoken to another in years. Sometimes, whatever caused the dispute has long been forgotten, but the inability for each to say "I'm sorry" continues the feud. Advent provides the opportunity to reach out and heal wounds. As we share in the Eucharist—the bread of life—this Sunday, let us reflect on any old wounds that need to be healed in our lives, and resolve to do so.

Extension

•Create a ritual that your family or students can use to ask forgiveness for the slights and hurts that have occurred throughout the year. Use this as a way to begin your Christmas festivities.

•Families in the parish can gather to share a time of forgiveness and healing with a reconciliation service. The service could be ended by sharing of the oplatek with each other.

•If your parish does not distribute oplatek at Christmas, you can get the oplatek wafer by writing to: Franciscan Friars, c/o Franciscan Center, Pulaski, Wisconsin 54162. A donation to help the Franciscan missions is greatly appreciated in return. You can also use other ethnic breads for your reconciliation celebration.

•Write to someone with whom you have not been in contact for awhile. If you can, send him or her a piece of oplatek as a sign of friendship and love. Or send along some symbolic item that represents your connectedness to them.

OXEN

Origin

Oxen are thought to have been part of St. Francis's original crèche in Italy in 1223. A popular story tells how an ox, laying in the stable beside the baby Jesus, warmed him with his breath on

that first Christmas night. Oxen are a symbol of humility; the evangelist Luke is sometimes depicted as an ox.

The charming legend of the ox cake traces back to Herefordshire, England. Here Christmas revelers would carry a bowl of wassail into the cow barn and drink toasts to all the farm animals. At some point during the festivities, a big, round cake with a hole in the center would be placed on the horn of an ox, who would then, as expected, toss it off. If the cake landed behind the ox, it brought good luck for the new year to the farmer's wife; if it landed in front, the luck was claimed by the estate steward.

Connection

Oxen have historically been used as work animals because of their strength. All of us do some type of work every day. Yet what is the ultimate goal of that work—to earn money, or use our talents, or bring justice to others? No matter what the immediate purpose of our effort, the long range goal must be to further God's work through ours.

Oxen work in relationship with people and machines. Likewise, God's goals are achieved when we work in relationship with others for the good of all creation. Work is the means by which we do our part to promote justice and love in the world.

Extension

•The ox's cake may have been like our doughnuts, bundt cakes, sweet rolls, or angel food cakes. As you eat one of those items during Advent, think of how the ox kept the baby Jesus warm without ever being asked.

•As part of your daily prayer during Advent, say these words: *I thank you, God, for the ability to work. Help me to follow your will in all that I do today, and may my efforts better the lives of others in some small way.*

•In countries where they are still used as beasts of burden, oxen wear a yoke over their shoulders in order to be hooked to a cart or plow. When your own burdens begin to wear you down this Advent, stand up straight and quietly pray, *There is no problem so big and heavy that God and I can't handle it.*

PIES

Origin

The English were famous for making pies out of just about any ingredient that could be baked: suet, sugar, apples, molasses, currants, peacock meat, mutton, and more. In fact, an old saying around England was "The devil himself dare not appear during Christmas for fear of being baked in a pie."

In England, pies were once shaped into ovals, with a small figure of the baby Jesus placed on top, as a reminder of the manger where Jesus lay. Later, the Puritans forbade oval pies and ruled that pies be shaped into circles so as not to remind people of the manger.

Connection

The traditional pie shape was changed at Christmas to encourage people to reflect on the mystery of the Incarnation. This shape was changed, however, because of its Christian symbolism. How often do we reshape our focus so our Christian values become known to others? What people help us to change, whether they are aware of this or not?

Extension

• Bake a pie to share with your family or friends, or with someone who would enjoy a special treat. Find a small figure of the baby Jesus and put it on top of the pie, along with a card that tells about oval pies and Jesus in the manger.

• Create a special food to become a family tradition. Talk about favorite foods, and see how some of these can be incorporated into your family tradition.

• As a group, talk about ways that can change the direction of the organization. Who or what would help with the change?

• Discuss the causes of violence on a local, national, and global level, and decide on one change that can lessen the violence.

PLUM PUDDING

Origin

Plum pudding is a traditional English Christmas food that has been around for hundreds of years. Before the 17th century, this pudding was called "hackin," because the ingredients were chopped before being mixed into the pie.

Plum pudding originally did not have plums in it at all. It was filled with grapes, meat broth, chopped cow tongue, wine, and spice, and often had silver coins baked into it. The person who received the silver coins in their pudding would make the pudding for the next celebration, and would be especially blessed during the coming year.

Even today, the plum pudding is presented with great ceremony on Christmas morning. It is covered with brandy, set on fire, and paraded into the dining room.

Connection

Many ethnic groups make certain foods for particular holidays and holy days. These types of practices help emphasize the "specialness" of the day. Take some time during Advent to reflect on the special moments that give life to our hopes and help create memories.

Extension

• When extending invitations to family members and friends who will be gathering for Christmas dinner or a get together, ask each one to write down a custom or tradition that is part of their family. You can read a few of these when you are all together, and perhaps even incorporate one or two customs into the day's celebration. Before next year, take some time to type these customs and put them into a booklet to be given to each family.

• Make a different flavor pudding on one night during each of the four weeks of Advent. Put a bean or whole nut into the pudding. The one who finds it can then be given a special privilege for the day.

• Have students tell their classmates about a Christmas custom their family enjoys.

POINSETTIA

Origin

The poinsettia was named after Dr. Joel Robert Poinsett, the first United States ambassador to Mexico. He brought these plants to the U.S. from Mexico, where he then began to raise them in his South Carolina greenhouse.

One Mexican legend tells of a young girl who wanted to visit the Nativity crib. But she was poor, and had no gift for the infant Jesus, so she sat outside the church where the Nativity scene stood and cried. Suddenly, a figure appeared and pointed to some nearby weeds. The figure told the little girl to take the weeds to the baby Jesus, and said that the gift itself was not as important as the love that caused it to be given.

The girl picked some of the weeds, and began to walk toward the church. As she walked, the green leaves of the weeds became bright red flowers, turning into what we now call the poinsettia. With a huge smile, the girl ran to the crib and presented the flowers to the baby Jesus.

To this day, poinsettias are a popular Christmas flower. Because of its starlike shape, the people of Mexico call the poinsettia the "flower of the holy night."

Connection

This story of the poinsettia reminds us of the importance our motives in giving a gift. Any gift given with the right intention is blessed and holy. The intention gives the gift a beauty that far surpasses the material value of the gift. The miracle of changing weeds to flowers occurs each time we give the gift of forgiveness.

Extension

•Place a poinsettia in the center of your family table or in the middle of your classroom. Talk about the poinsettia legend, and how the gift of love transformed the weeds into beautiful flowers. Have family members or students tell about a gift they received that was given out of love, and how it changed their lives.

•Copy the legend about the origin of the poinsettia, attach it to a small poinsettia plant, and give it to someone who will be spending Christmas alone this year.

•Use the poinsettia as the focus of a family or classroom ritual of reconciliation. To start, cover a poinsettia plant with a brown bag. Then lead the group through a litany like the one below:

Leader: For the times we have not been honest...

Response: *Lord, forgive us.*

Leader: For the times we have been mean or unkind...

Response: *Lord, forgive us.*

Leader: For the times we have neglected our brothers and sisters who are in need...

Response: *Lord, forgive us.*

Continue this litany by adding your own petitions. Then, have all say an act of contrition together, or use this prayer:

Lord Jesus, we prepare our hearts to welcome you once again this Christmas. Forgive us for the times when we have not acted in love, and help us always to remember that you are our light and our hope. Fill our hearts with your joy, and let us share your peace with one another. Amen.

Now remove the brown bag. End your reconciliation ritual with a group blessing and hug for everyone.

•Find food for thought in Isaiah 40:6–8 and 1 Peter 1:24.

POSADAS

Origin

Posadas is a Spanish word meaning "shelter." This tradition is most often attributed to the Hispanic people; however, the basics of the tradition are also celebrated in other European countries.

The posadas reenacts the story of Mary and Joseph, as they searched for a place to stay in Bethlehem. For nine days before Christmas, people of a certain neighborhood or group would gather in a different home each evening. The group would process from room to room, carrying candles and praying to be given entrance. Two of the group would represent Mary and Joseph, and ask for hospitality; at all doors except the last, they were turned away. At the last room, which was set with a manger scene, all would be welcomed in and the evening would end with a party.

The posadas is still practiced in much of the southwestern United States, as well as in parts of South and Central America. Usually, the procession from house to house is done on one evening, nine days before Christmas. Another popular feature of the posadas is the lighting of *luminarias*, small candles set in brown paper bags filled with sand. The luminarias are placed along the route of the procession to light the way for the travelers.

In some European countries, scripture stories about the Nativity would be acted out in play form. Often live Nativity scenes were set in front of churches and other public places where people could pass by and enjoy.

58

Connection

Our lives are a constant journey. There are times when we know exactly where we are headed; at other times, we may wander aimlessly, trying to find direction. The posadas is a celebration of two people, Joseph and Mary, who searched for a place to stay. In today's world, full of people who are displaced in one way or another, the posadas offers an opportunity to reflect on where we are going in life.

Extension

•Plan to hold a posadas in your neighborhood. Let several houses nearby (nine would be ideal) know in advance of your plans. Then, on the appointed night, form a procession and knock on the door of the first house, asking for shelter. After being turned away, proceed to the next house, and so on, until you reach the last house. There, all are welcomed in. Have a small party, with refreshments and the singing of carols.

As a variation during Advent, plan a posadas celebration with as many classrooms as possible during one day of your religious education program. Set up a plan based on the one above.

•With your family or class, read a different Nativity story from scripture during each week of Advent.

Week One: Matthew 1:18–35
Week Two: Mark 1:1–13 (a prelude to Jesus' public ministry)
Week Three: Luke 2:1–20
Week Four: John 1:1–18

•Set out your Nativity set at the beginning of Advent. As you take the figures out of the box, tell the Nativity story so that your children become familiar with it.

•Place the manger figures far from the crèche, then each day during Advent, move them closer. (You might want to do this before the evening meal, or at breakfast.) Keep the figure of Jesus hidden until Christmas Eve, then bring it in with special ceremony.

•With your family or class during this Advent season, plan to adopt a homeless family and provide Christmas gifts for them. Find out if there are ways you can help them find permanent shelter. Or, collect food and other supplies for a local food bank that helps the homeless.

SPIDERS

Origin

You might not think that spiders have a place in the Christmas story, but stories about spiders and Christmas are quite popular in Germany. One legend relates that on Christmas Eve, families allowed the animals to come inside to see all of the beautiful decorations. There was one exception, however; the spiders had to stay outside because the house was clean, and spiders had a way of spinning webs everywhere. The spiders did not like this, so they complained to the Christ child.

Jesus felt sorry for the spiders, and late on Christmas Eve, he let all the spiders into the houses. The spiders became so excited that they traveled all over, admiring the beautifully decorated Christmas trees. As they traveled, they left trails of web. Jesus noticed the spider webs, and changed them all into beautiful threads of silver and glitter. In the morning, when the family awoke, they saw that the tree was covered with wonderful, silvery threads. Today, we use tinsel to remind us of this delightful tale.

Connection

Spiders are often considered less than wonderful creatures. They manage to get into places you wish they wouldn't. Some people are like that, too, people who may be different than we and whom we just wish might go away. Yet all people, like spiders, need to have others discover their value and gifts. This Advent, stop and see the goodness in someone whom you may previously have ignored.

Extension

•Get a picture book from the library about spiders, and read it with your class or family. Take time to appreciate the uniqueness of each kind of spider. Notice their defense mechanisms, the way they move from place to place, what they eat, and other interesting facts about them.

•Create a spider ornament. Cut out one "bump" of an egg carton, and paint it black or brown. Attach four black or brown pipe cleaners through the bump to create eight legs, and with another pipe cleaner, create a head for the spider. Put glue on the legs and sprinkle with glitter. Attach a thread to the back of the spider, and suspend the ornament from the Christmas tree.

•Spiders are considered out of place in our homes. Our first impulse is to step on them or kill them in some other way. Yet all of creation is a gift from God. Practice gently moving insects, spiders, and other creatures back outside rather than killing them. In this way we can better learn to respect all of life.

•Place some tinsel on your Christmas tree when you are ready to decorate, and also on some ordinary items around the house. Use this as a reminder that the ordinary is important, and can be beautiful, too.

STAR

Origin
The star has been a source of guidance from as far back as we know. Sailors used the stars to help them keep their ships on course. Scouts are shown how to find the North Star to guide them in the right direction if they get lost while hiking or camping. It can be argued that the most famous star, particularly in the Western world, is the star that the three Wise Men followed to find the baby Jesus.

In medieval times, it was the custom to have a Nativity pageant which became part of the liturgy. Eventually, the pageants were banned from liturgy, because Herod was played as a wild man who threw things and beat other participants.

Over time, another type of play was introduced by the Franciscans. In this scriptural reenactment, three elegantly dressed people depicting the Wise Men would ride though the streets of the village carrying golden cups filled with gold, frankincense, and myrrh. When they reached the church, they would leave their horses at the door and enter with great pomp to present their gifts to the infant Jesus. After the Reformation, these plays were banned.

Today, the image of the star is the focus of many manger scenes and is a popular symbol for Christmas ornaments and decorations. In the Philippines, people use lanterns made out of paper, sticks, and yarn as Christmas stars and hang them in the window.

Connection

Stars hold a sense of mystery. They can cause one to pause, to be quiet, and to wonder. These are the very same words we use when talking about prayer. Take a moment to pause and to step out of the ordinary. Be very quiet, and listen to the words of God. Wonder at the mystery that surrounds our lives.

Extension

•Give each member of your family or class a star made out of shiny, bright paper, decorated with glitter. (You can also use the recipe for cinnamon stars given below.) Invite them to think of all the ways they are light for one another. Place these stars on a bulletin board or on a bare branch in the middle of the table during the Advent season. At Christmas, place the stars on the Christmas tree.

A variation of this ritual would be to present a star to those who have been "stars" for you during the past year. You can write a brief note of thanks on the back of the star, or a prayer for blessings in the coming year.

•Use this recipe to make cinnamon stars (nonedible):

   1 cup ground cinnamon
   4 tablespoons craft glue
   3/4 cup water

Mix ingredients together and refrigerate for two hours. Roll to 1/4 inch thickness and cut out shapes with a star cookie cutter. Using a drinking straw, make a hole in the top to hang the ornament. Dry at room temperature for two days, turning twice each day, or place on a cookie sheet and bake in a 250° oven for several hours.

• As a group, go for a night walk and observe the stars. Watch how they radiate and glow, filling the sky with brightness and warmth. Praise God for the gift of stars.

• Read the story "The Hermitage," found in the book *The Quest for the Flaming Pearl,* by Edward Hays.

• Find food for thought in Matthew 2:1–10 and 1 Corinthians 15: 35–41.

STRAW

Origin

Straw has become a mainstay in Christmas traditions throughout the world because of its association with a manger as the birthplace of Jesus. Swedish families decorate their Christmas trees with straw figures, and also put a sheaf of grain on a pole to make a Christmas tree for the birds.

Similarly, Norwegian people put sheaves of straw on their lawns for the birds to come and eat. Some believe that if there are many sparrows in the sheaves on Christmas Day, the family will have a good yield of corn. If only one sparrow is in the sheaves, however, it means that a member of the family will die during the coming year.

Wheat is planted on household plates in Belgium on December 10. By Christmas day, enough has grown so that it makes a small wheat field to use as a decoration for the windowsill. In Lithuania, Christmas trees are decorated with straw bird cages and stars made of straw. When the first star shines on Christmas Eve in Poland, families spread straw over the floor, under the tablecloth, and under the dishes to make the room look like a stable. One chair is left empty at the table as a reminder that Jesus is coming.

Russian-American families go to grandmother's house on Christmas Eve, where they kneel on the floor for an hour and pray. Then the youngest child is placed in a basket of straw, symbolizing the birth of the Christ child. Spanish children fill their shoes with straw and set them out for the camels of the three kings. The straw is then replaced with gifts.

Connection
Straw provides comfort and warmth to animals, and is a source of food for them, as well. It reminds us of the importance of simple things. Our lives are made up of small actions, just like a bale has many stems of straw. Most of us won't be famous and recognized by many people, but we can be genuine and truly Christian in our day to day activities.

Extension
• In your home or classroom at the beginning of Advent, plant some grain seeds in a dish. As you care for them, think of growing spiritually in preparation for the birth of Jesus.

• Find a small, empty Nativity crib or make one out of popsicle sticks. Then find some straw (dried grasses or weeds from outside can do nicely), and put it next to the crib. Ask family members to put in a piece of straw each time they do a good deed during Advent. At Christmas, the crib will be well-padded and ready for the baby Jesus.

• Set some straw out in a place where family members or students can see it. Each time you pass by pray a short prayer, such as "I love you, Jesus," or "Help me, Jesus, to do right."

• When there is straw there has been grain. Give a box of cereal or pasta to the local food bank. You can also collect boxes of the same to give to a food bank during Advent as a family or class project.

• Find food for thought in Isaiah 65:25 and 1 Corinthians 3:12.

TREE DECORATIONS

Origin

The custom of decorating trees for Christmas likely derived from the Roman celebration of Saturnalia, during which trees were covered with ornaments and candles. Yet decorating a tree for Christmas did not become common until the middle of the 19th century, in Germany. This tradition was then brought to the United States with the European immigrants.

Fruits have long been used as popular tree decorations. The Christian origin for this may come from the story of the Garden of Eden, which tells how the fir tree had both flowers and fruits until Eve took off one of the fruits. From that time on, the fir tree grew only needles, until it blossomed again on the evening of the Nativity.

Candles (now electric lights) are another common tree decoration. Their use could have been in imitation of the Jewish celebration of Hanukkah, the festival of lights. In western Germany, families arranged candles on steps or shelves to make a pyramid shape. It was common to see Christmas trees decorated with hundreds of wax candles to note the coming of Christ as the light of the world.

Pastry decorations, similar in shape to communion bread, were once commonly hung on the tree. These were replaced by pastries and candies as symbols of the sweet fruit of Christ's redemption. The food decorations were often shared with carolers.

One German legend attributes decorating Christmas trees with lights to Martin Luther. According to the story, as Luther walked home one night, he noticed how the stars glistened on the trees. When he got home, he cut down a fir tree and decorated it with candles to imitate the natural beauty of the stars. In spite of this legend, the first use of candles for tree decorations isn't recorded until the 17th century.

Other tree decorations came about as cultural expressions. The following countries are noted for their distinct decorations: Sweden, painted wooden ornaments and straw figures; Czechoslovakia, painted eggshells and glass ornaments; Germany, glass trinkets; Norway, golden nuts, cookies, and a three-pronged candle on top; Japan, tiny fans and paper lanterns; Hungary, small bits of hard candy wrapped in white paper to look like snowflakes; and China, paper flowers, paper chains, and cotton snowflakes.

The process of decorating the tree also holds many special customs in different parts of the world. In some Scandinavian homes, families share fruit soup and a rice pudding in which there is an almond. The person who gets the almond is promised a year of good luck, but must make a Christmas tree ornament for whomever finds the almond during next year's festival.

Connection

Tree decorations hold meaning to the people who use them. The same is true of how we decorate our surroundings during Christmas. What do our decorations say about who we are, and about how we are living our lives? Are there signs of Christ and Christianity around our homes? Do our words and our actions reflect our faith?

Extension

•Have a family discussion about how your home is decorated. Perhaps during Advent, one particular item could be put away, leaving a blank space reserved for Jesus when he comes.

Before you put out your decorations, review them and see what message your decorations communicate to others. Maybe this is a good time to sort them out, and add some that are more reflective of who you are.

•Give your home or classroom a multicultural flavor this year by using some of the ideas from other countries found above to decorate your tree. Or, celebrate Jesus, the light of the world, by having only lights on the tree.

•Make tree ornaments out of gingerbread or sugar cookie dough. Before you bake the cookies, make a hole through which to put the ribbon to hang on the tree. Decorate the ornaments when baked, protect them with plastic wrap before hanging on the tree, and give them to holiday guests.

WASSAIL

Origin

Wassail comes from the words *was haile*, which means "be of good health." This custom originated with the English, who would toast each other with mugs of a hot, spiced cider with a fruity apple base.

On Christmas Eve, the wassail bowl was carried from home to home, where everyone would help themselves to a mug while toasting each other's good health. Whatever punch remained was often poured over the roots of the best apple tree, and a shotgun blast fired through the tree branches in hopes that the apple harvest would be good in the coming year.

Another popular Christmas tradition treats carolers to a cup of wassail as they go singing from house to house. After all have finished drinking, the farmers take the bowls of wassail to the barnyards and toast the health of their cattle, bees, fruit trees, and fields.

Connection

Often when we talk about health, we mean the condition of our bodies. Although physical health is important, spiritual health is also an essential part of being a full human being. Advent can be our time to have a complete spiritual examination. We can review the wounds which need healing, and at the same time, reflect on the wrongs we may have caused another. Let us call on God to be our spiritual doctor, and help us through our spiritual examination. We can then develop a plan to improve our spiritual health.

Extension

•Gather together a group, and go caroling throughout the neighborhood during one night of the Christmas season. Be sure to sing the traditional English carol, "Here We Come A-Wassailing." Or, with your family or class, visit a nursing home and sing a few carols for the residents there.

•Invite your neighbors over for a mug of wassail, making sure to offer a toast to good health for all present. Make a wassail punch using the following recipe:

1 gallon apple cider
2 cinnamon sticks
1 whole nutmeg
5-6 whole cloves
stainless steel or enamel pot, at least 6-quart capacity

Put all the ingredients in a pot. Bring to a simmer, but do not boil. Simmer for 30 minutes. Serve warm.

•Visit a hospital and offer a sign of joy to patients who may not have other visitors.

YULE LOG

Origin

The custom of burning a yule log is said to have started in the northern countries of Sweden and Norway. In pre-Christian times, the Scandinavian people believed in the "world tree," a tree with one root in heaven, one in hell, and one on earth. When they became Christians, they burned a tree each year to remind them of their history, as well as to symbolize the end of old beliefs.

This tradition was carried into other parts of Europe. Selecting a tree for burning became a cause for celebration, and much singing and dancing took place as the tree was chopped down and dragged home. Some people would prepare a log on Candlemas Day (February 2), then store and dry it to be ready for the next Christmas.

The yule log would be lit on Christmas Day, and the celebration of Christmas would continue as long as the yule log was burning. For this reason, it was important to select as big and thick a log as possible. The burning yule log served as an image of light and warmth in the season of cold and dark.

Many local customs arose around the yule log. Among them was the belief that it was unlucky to burn all of the yule log, so some of it had to be saved to use in the following year's fire. Another practice involved burning any Christmas plants and remnants of the yule log still left on February 2; the ashes would then be sprinkled over the fields.

Today, yule logs are often decorated with evergreens and bows, and placed beside the fireplace. Some people save these logs for special occasions or use them as the start of their Christmas fire. Yule logs are often given as gifts that bring good luck, warmth, and friendship to the receiver.

Connection

Fire is a powerful symbol. It can bring warmth and be used as a way to cook food. Yet it can also cause destruction through nature or through the carelessness of humans. Let us use the fire from the yule log as a symbol of the power of God's love, a love that can redeem but that also knows justice.

Extension

•Make yule logs from old Christmas tree trunks. Cut the trunk into 18- to 24-inch lengths, and store them for a year so that they dry out. During Advent of the following year, decorate the logs with ribbon and fresh evergreens. Give them as gifts to people that have been helpful to you during the year.

•Volunteer to help at a nature center one day during Advent. Make plans ahead of time to gather wood, clear areas that are in need of attention, or some other task.

•Read aloud *The Giving Tree*, by Shel Silverstein.

•The Native American people have a custom of putting food by a tree that has given them shelter. Fertilize the trees in your yard so they will have a good beginning for a new season. Put food out for the birds who live in the trees.

•This Christmas, give the gift of a tree to someone who loves trees. Attach a card saying that you will plant the tree for them in the spring, when it becomes possible to do so.

LENT
&
EASTER

LENT

In the northern hemisphere, Lent begins when all is in darkness. The days are short and the nights are long; the whole world seems to be asleep. As Lent passes, the days grow longer and signs of spring begin to appear.

In the early Church, Lent was a time of preparation for those who were planning to become Christians. The catechumens were held to strict disciplines during Lent: they could not bathe, and had to fast each day until sunset. Many of the other members of the Christian community chose to take part in these practices as well, and kept the same disciplines as the catechumens.

During spring in those days, it was necessary for people to eat all the perishable foods that remained from the winter larder, including such items as meat, cheese, eggs, and butter. The cold had provided natural refrigeration, but as the earth warmed, these foods began to spoil, and there was little to eat until spring vegetables began to grow. This made fasting during Lent somewhat of a natural practice.

Over the years, people went from one meal late in the afternoon and only water otherwise, to small meals during the day to sustain their energy for the manual labor most people were engaged in. In the nineteenth century, one main meal and two light meals became the norm for fasting.

The duration of Lent—40 days—was determined in the 4th century. The number "40" recalled the 40 days Moses spent on Mount Sinai before receiving the commandments, as well as the 40 years the Hebrew people wandered in the desert before reaching the promised land. Christian scriptures tell how Jesus fasted in the desert for 40 days before beginning his public ministry.

Lent ends with the start of the Triduum, three holy days that mark the death, burial, and resurrection of Jesus. The Triduum begins with evening Mass on Holy Thursday, and ends with vespers (evening prayer) on Easter Sunday.

EASTER

Easter is considered the most important of all Christian feasts. Many people celebrate this special morning with sunrise services, and an old legend tells how on Easter morning, the sun jumps to celebrate the resurrection. It was believed that the rays of sun coming through the clouds were the angels dancing on this joyful day.

The word "Easter" has been attributed to several sources. The Venerable Bede wrote that the name came from Eastre, an Anglo-Saxon spring goddess. Another explanation is that "easter" was a misinterpretation of the Latin word *albis*—translated into old High German as *eostarun*—which means "white vestments" and refers to the garments worn by the catechumens. Also, Easter begins with the word "east," the direction of the rising sun.

Easter is not a fixed feast. It is celebrated on the first Sunday after the first full moon that follows the first day of spring. During the 18th century, it was the custom in some places for the pastor to tell many funny stories during the Easter Sunday Mass. This was to bring back the laughter that had been put away during the lenten season.

Easter is called "the great day" by the Ukrainian and Russian people. The people of Hungary call it "the feast of meat" because after fasting, meat can again be eaten. In Ireland and England, people place a pan of water in an east window, and watch the sun dance in the water.

In France, Easter was once celebrated at the beginning of a new year. This was the time that prisoners, as well as slaves, were released. If someone was involved in a feud with another person, the feud would be ended on Easter.

Easter has many symbols, customs, and traditions that focus on new life. We will explore some of these in the following pages.

ALLELUIA

Origin

"Alleluia" is a powerful word, for which there is no substitute. This word, sometimes written as "Hallelujah," is interpreted as a cry of joy meaning "praise the Lord." It is heard with the greatest eloquence and emphasis during the Easter season, as part of Christian liturgies.

The Alleluia is silenced at Mass during the entire lenten season, not said again until the Easter Vigil Mass on Holy Saturday night. In both Russia and Poland, the traditional Easter greeting is "Wesolego Alleluia," or "Happy Alleluia!"

Connection

Alleluia is a unique word that has special meaning during Easter. Each of us is equally special in the whole of creation. The relationship between God and each of us is so unique that no single person or group of persons can match it. Let us celebrate the wonder of our own special relationship with God that causes us to say "Alleluia," "Praise the Lord!"

Extension

•Make a brightly colored paper or cloth banner with words of praise on it, such as Alleluia, new life, and joy. Hide your banner in a box or some other place on Ash Wednesday, and take it out on Easter morning as part of your celebration.

• Teach your family or students the words to an Alleluia hymn, whether a traditional one or something contemporary. Sing it at mealtimes, or at the start of classes throughout the Easter season.

•Cut out the letters of the word "Alleluia" from colorful paper, and make a mobile of them to hang up on Easter. You can also paint "Alleluia!" on a few of your Easter eggs.

•Listen to the "Hallelujah Chorus," from Handel's *Messiah*.

•Send out Easter cards to your family and friends that say, "We wish you a happy alleluia."

ASHES

Origin

Ashes have long been used to symbolize penance and humility. In Genesis 18:27, we read the prayer of Abraham: "I am bold to speak like this to my Lord, I who am dust and ashes."

The use of ashes as a Christian symbol was first noted around the 4th century. At this time, sinners would be marked with ashes, and temporarily expelled from the community for wrongs such as heresy, murder, adultery, and apostasy.

By the 7th century, this practice had evolved into a public Ash Wednesday ritual. Sinners were made to wear sackcloth and ashes, and made to live apart from their families for all of Lent. They could not enter the church, and were kept from speaking to others. They did penance, prayed, slept on the ground or a straw tick, and could not bathe or cut their hair. On Holy Thursday, they would be absolved from their sins and allowed to return home.

The parish ritual we now practice became the norm around the time of Pope Urban II (late 11th century). Today, a sign of the cross is traced on our foreheads with ashes made from last year's palms. The ashes symbolize the beginning of a holy season, a time for reflection and renewal.

Connection

Palms being changed into ashes is an apt sign for the meaning of Lent. It is a time to look at the habits, attitudes, and behaviors of our lives that may need to be changed. At the same time, we take steps to enhance the positive things we are doing. God calls us to be new creations, to let go of our old selves and put on the new. Lent gives us the spiritual opportunity to change; ashes remind us of this.

Extension

•Hold an Ash Wednesday ritual with your family. Have each member think of one attitude or behavior they would like to change to make family relations better. Write these down on last year's palms, then burn the palms. (Light some charcoal in a grill or other fireproof container—make sure to do this outside or in a well-protected and ventilated area—then burn the palms on the charcoal. Palms are difficult to burn, so make sure they are dry and the fire is hot.) Sign each other on the forehead with ashes from the burnt palms.

• At the start of Lent, have students write down on small pieces of paper something they would like to change about themselves during the coming lenten season. Collect the papers and put them in a jar with a lid on it. Keep the jar visible during Lent as a reminder that this is the season of change and renewal.

• Have each member of your family select a favorite canned food. Remove the labels, and burn them in a fireproof container. Put the ashes in an empty can, and place in a conspicuous place as a reminder to change eating habits through the lenten season.

BASKETS

Origin

Baskets have many uses: to serve in, to carry things, and to store in. Many people use them as decorations. Jesus provided baskets of bread in the story of the multiplication of the loaves and fishes. Children today look forward to finding baskets filled with candy and other treats on Easter morning.

In the countries of Eastern Europe, special baskets were set aside just for Easter. These baskets would be filled with foods for the Easter meal, such as ham, bread, salt, butter, eggs, and perhaps a special Easter cake. Each basket would also have a candle in it, as a symbol of the radiance of the resurrected Christ.

The food baskets would be brought to church on Holy Saturday morning to be blessed. After the blessing, the baskets were brought outside, and the contents spread on the grass in front of the basket for all to see. Of course, each basket had in it many intricately painted eggs called *pysanky*. These were exchanged with friends and relatives before all would return home to prepare for the Easter meal, traditionally eaten on Holy Saturday evening.

Connection

Baskets are used to carry and to store, as well as for decoration. Baskets can be plain and simple, or elaborate. They can be handmade from materials close at hand or woven by someone in a far off country. What baskets in our lives need to be prepared in order to hold the Easter message?

Extension

• Place an Easter basket in a prominent place at the beginning of Lent. Have family members or students write activities on a piece of paper that can be done as a group or individually during Lent. Place these in the basket. Each time your family or class gathers together, take out a slip of paper and follow the suggestion written on it.

• Another basket can be put in the middle of the family table, or on the front desk of your classroom. Several times during the weeks of Lent, invite everyone to think of some good things they have done for others or for themselves. Write these actions down on strips of paper, and place them in the basket. On Easter, decorate the basket with colorful ribbons and put painted Easter eggs inside.

BUTTERFLY

Origin

Of all of the symbols Christians use to represent new life on Easter, the butterfly is one of the most well-known. Throughout Christian history it has stood as a strong symbol of breaking out from the old life to the new.

In the language of Easter, the caterpillar represents life, and the cocoon, the tomb where Jesus lay for three days after he died. The butterfly itself is a symbol of Christ's resurrection, new life where there seemed to be only death.

Connection

If a cocoon is opened early, the butterfly will die because it did not develop strength by struggling to break out of the cocoon. Perhaps God lets us struggle sometimes within our own cocoons, because God knows that by our stress and battle we become stronger persons. Thus, we are more willing to take risks that further the kingdom. If we include God in our struggle through prayer, our relationship with God will be strengthened, as well.

Extension

•During Lent, make a caterpillar out of modeling clay and wrap it in a cocoon of brown paper. Display this in your home or classroom as a sign of waiting for Easter Sunday, and the hope of new life through Jesus Christ.

•Make butterflies out of materials such as wallpaper, clothespins, folded paper, pipe cleaners, fabric, or crushed egg shells pasted on cardboard. Use them as decorations for Easter and during the Easter season. Large-size butterflies can be placed outside in trees as part of your Easter celebration.

•Make or buy small butterflies and take them to people who are hospitalized or confined to their homes. You might include a brief paragraph on a card about the symbolism of the butterfly, or simply tell them how butterflies represent the cycle of life, death, and resurrection.

•Use table napkins that are decorated with butterflies for your Easter table.

•With your family or students, read aloud the book *Hope for the Flowers*, by Trina Paulus.

•Pray for persons who are forced to stay in cocoons because they are political prisoners.

CROSS

Origin

The cross has long been a common sign in the history of humankind. Perhaps the earliest cross was made of two sticks when they were rubbed together to make fire. Its ends point in four directions: north, south, east, and west. The four ends can also symbolize the four elements of the world (earth, water, fire, and air), or the four dimensions of the universe (height, length, width, breadth).

The cross of Christ is seen as the tree of life, a sign of love and a symbol of Jesus' victory over death and evil. From the earliest days of the church, the cross has been one of its most central symbols. It is found in the catacombs, sometimes by itself but often in combination with other images. Many different shapes and designs of crosses have evolved, but the Christian symbolism of salvation, redemption, and atonement remain the same.

The sign of the cross is used to bless people, places, and things. In Sweden, a cross is drawn on the nose of cattle to protect them from the witch who supposedly comes between Holy Thursday and Easter. Likewise, a cross painted on the door of a home or barn provides safety for the people and animals who live within.

In the Blue Ridge section of Virginia, one can find small stones shaped like crosses. Legend tells that when the fairies in Virginia heard about the crucifixion, they wept. Their tears fell to the ground and turned into cross-shaped stones. The fairy stones of Virginia are said to give magical powers to anyone who carries them.

One of the many beautiful Easter legends tells how the wood from the dogwood tree was used to make the cross on which Christ was crucified. Originally, the dogwood was a strong and mighty tree like the oak. But after it was used to make the cross, Jesus promised that the dogwood would never again be straight enough to be used in that way; it would be thin and crooked, with blossoms shaped like a cross.

Another legend relates a branch from the Tree of Knowledge was planted on Adam's grave. A tree grew there over time, but Solomon had it cut down to use in building the temple in Jerusalem. When the wood was found unsuitable, however, it was used to build a bridge across a brook. Later, the wood was buried in the pool of Bethseda. At the time of the Jesus' crucifixion, it floated up and was used for the wood of the cross.

Connection

The cross identifies Christians as believers in Jesus. Yet, too often when we reflect on the cross, we think only of the suffering of Jesus. We need to remember that what follows is the resurrection. We also should know that a new way of life follows each small "death" in our own lives: a disappointment, a failure, a conflict, or any situation in which we are called to let go.

Although Lent can sometimes be a somber and serious time, God always brings out the hope, the new life, and the joy that we have because of Jesus' death and resurrection. Holding on to the past is like holding on to death. We need to grow and move forward with true hope in what Jesus promised to all who believe.

Extension

•In your home or in class, make a large cross out of paper. Cut out pictures of suffering and sin from a magazine or newspaper. Glue these onto one side of the cross. Then, as Lent goes on, find pictures of new life and kind actions. Glue these on the other side of the cross to show that out of suffering comes new life.

•Make small crosses out of a variety of materials: twigs, nails, popsicle sticks, matches, cardboard. Put them in places in your home or classroom where a cross wouldn't ordinarily be found: on the television, at someone's desk, on the chalkboard, near the telephone, or on the car dashboard.

•If you have saved a piece of the trunk from your Christmas tree, make a lenten cross with it, or use another tree trunk. Cut the log into two pieces, and fit together in the shape of a cross. Drill seven holes in the cross, and place five purple candles, one pink candle, and a white candle in the holes. On each Sunday of Lent, light one of the candles (the pink one is lit on the fourth Sunday, and the white on Easter morning).

•Cut a cross out of cardboard and make some flowers out of construction or tissue paper. Every time someone in your family or class does a good deed or makes a special sacrifice during Lent, he or she can put a flower on the cross.

•With your family or students, read aloud the book, *The Tale of Three Trees*, by Angela Elwell Hunt (Lion Publishing).

•Lift a heavy piece of lumber and hold it on your shoulders for a few minutes. Imagine carrying it a long distance, as Jesus did with his cross.

CROWN

Origin

Crowns denote sovereignty and kingship, and have long been used as a symbol of Jesus. Some say that Jesus takes all of our years, sweeps them up into eternity, and wears time like a crown.

In the Gospels, a crown of thorns is placed on Jesus' head to mock his claim of kingship. One legend says that the crown of thorns was made from the branches of an acacia tree. This tree was believed to have been brought out of Egypt by the Hebrews, and its wood used to build both the Tabernacle and the Ark of the Covenant.

The crown of thorns may have actually been a wreath of wild rose canes, which are native to Palestine. Roses symbolize love, beauty, and youth, and are associated with the Holy Family. Their existence can be traced back five thousand years or more. In many parts of Europe, legend has it that the flowers of the wild rose were originally white, but changed to red as the blood of Jesus flowed down from the crown of thorns on his head.

Connection

Jesus was mocked and crowned with thorns because of what other people thought he was. Do we do the same to those whom we do not understand? We are all equal in the eyes of God, and it is unlikely that God wants us to belittle any part of creation. Think about persons who may be odd by the standards of society. Reflect on how God lives in each of these people in the same way that God lives in us.

Extension

•Take a winter walk, and try to find some thorny branches. Fashion them into a wreath which can be used as a centerpiece in your home or classroom.

•Make a crown out of cardboard for each member of your family or class, and decorate them with markers, foil, glitter, and the like. Have each person put a crown on his or her head, and celebrate their talents, gifts, and abilities.

•Give a rose to someone who may need to have a bright spot in his or her day.

•With your family or students, talk about behaviors that can be thorns in life, such as loudness, mean habits, name-calling, or rudeness. Ask each person to look at themselves, and find one way in which their behavior may be a thorn to others. Resolve to work on correcting one thorn during each week of Lent.

•Pray that you might understand and accept those persons whom you call "thorns in your side."

•Find food for thought in Revelation 14:14.

EASTER BREADS

Origin

Bread is mentioned in the Bible nearly 330 times, which suggests its value for spiritual life as well as for physical sustenance. Easter breads are symbolic of Jesus, who is the living bread. On Holy Thursday, Jesus took bread, blessed it, and passed it around the table to his friends. He told those present that they should do the same in remembrance of him, and to share this bread of life with others.

Easter breads contain wonderful, rich ingredients and are often highly decorated. In eastern European countries, there is usually an admonishment to use only the ingredients listed for the bread: margarine may not be used for butter, or whole eggs for egg yolks. The Easter bread must be made from the very best ingredients.

Kneading the dough is another important step, and must be done with care and enough time to create the smooth, satiny dough necessary for the best bread.

Connection

Care and patience help make good bread. If a person hurries or takes a shortcut in making bread, it may end up tough, or heavy, or flat, perhaps not even edible. It also takes time to build relationships, both with God and with all of creation.

By hurrying, we can easily miss the beauty in nature, in events, and in other people as well as in ourselves. Like bread ingredients, all of our experiences and encounters interact to make us who we are, but we must take the time to let them affect us. God never hurries us, but is always ready for us in our own time.

Extension

•Invite your students to bring in their favorite bread to share with the other students in class. Talk about how each of the breads is different from the others, what cultures they may have come from or their varied tastes. Reflect on how bread is a common food that nourishes us.

•When eating bread with your family during Lent and Easter think of Jesus, the bread of life. Be aware of how bread provides sustenance, and how it fills the hungry.

• Use a sweet bread recipe to make *panne de Pasqua*, the bread of Easter. Divide the dough into three pieces, and roll each piece into a rope. Braid the three pieces and shape them into a wreath, pressing the ends together. Let the dough rise in a warm, dry place.

When the dough has risen, place five raw, washed eggs into the top of the braid. Bake the bread as directed. When it has baked and is cool, color the eggs with food coloring or egg dye, using a small paint brush. The three ropes are symbolic of the Trinity, while the five eggs are a reminder of the five wounds of Jesus.

EASTER MONDAY

Origin

Easter week was once called "white week," or "the week of new garments." This was to acknowledge the white robes, symbols of new life, worn by those who were being baptized at the Easter vigil.

During past times in England, a favorite custom was "lifting." On Easter Monday, young men went from home to home in the village carrying a chair decorated with flowers. When a young woman sat in the chair, they lifted her into the air three times to bring her good luck. She then thanked the young men with money and a kiss. On the next day, it was the women's turn to lift the men in a chair. The lifting symbolized Jesus being "lifted" off the cross, and was also a sign of hope that the year's crops would grow tall.

In parts of Europe, Easter Monday is called "ducking Monday," and is a day for pushing friends into the water. In Hungary, boys sprinkle girls with perfume, and wish them good luck with sayings such as, "Now you will not wither away." The girls then give coins or colored Easter eggs to the boys.

Easter Monday is "the day of whipping" in Czechoslovakia. Boys braid willow branches into whips and decorate them with flowers and colored ribbons. Then they roam around town singing for eggs and "whipping" the village girls "so they won't be lazy or have fleas."

Families and friends go for long walks into fields and forests on Easter Monday in Europe, singing and dancing along the way. This tradition evolved from the Gospel story about two of Jesus' friends, walking to a village called Emmaus, near Jerusalem. Along the way, they were surprised by a man who suddenly appeared and walked along with them. Later, the two discovered that this man was the risen Christ.

The Easter kiss is a still a popular form of greeting, especially in Russia. Friends and even strangers hug and kiss when they meet, with a greeting of "Alleluia! Christ is risen!" and a response of "He is truly risen! Alleluia!"

Connection

Christians all over the world enjoy continuing the excitement and celebration of Easter into the following day. In our own lives, we all have momentous times: births, graduation, marriage, receiving school honors, or a promotion. After the event is over, we have photographs and other tokens to remind us of the day. We bury the souvenirs, yet resurrect them again and again to remind us of the joy. During this Easter season, we can use the Gospel stories of the resurrection to remind us of the joy of this wondrous event.

Extension

• Take an Emmaus walk on Easter Monday. Go to some place that has special meaning to you and your family, or to some place where you haven't gone for a while. Imagine that Jesus is walking along with you.

• In class after Easter, read the Gospel story about Jesus' friends on the road to Emmaus. Talk with your students about how the two men may have felt. How would the children feel if they discovered Jesus was walking along beside them?

• Plan your wardrobe to wear something white every day during the week after Easter. As you dress and undress, make a simple statement of thanksgiving and faith, such as "God, I thank you for giving me the gift of faith."

• Imitate the Russian custom by saying "Alleluia! Christ is risen!" to those persons you encounter on Easter Sunday, and in the days following. Ask them to respond with "He is truly risen. Alleluia!"

•Give a gift of perfume or toilet water to someone who would not expect it.

EGGS

Origin

Long before eggs took on Christian meaning, they were seen as a symbol of spring and fertility. The ancient Persians are said to have given each other colored eggs on the first day of spring. In China, it is still the custom to give a gift of eggs when a baby is born. Samoan people believe that the world began when Tangaloa-Langi, the Heavenly One, entered an egg and broke it to pieces, thus creating the earth.

Over time, as with many customs, the pagan interpretation was changed and a Christian meaning defined. The egg became a symbol of the tomb. As Jesus was laid in a tomb and then rose on Easter, so, too, new life comes forth from the egg which had seemed to be dead.

In times past, eggs were one of the foods that could not be eaten during Lent. This increased the importance of eggs as an Easter symbol, when the lenten fast would finally be over and eggs could once again be eaten.

Many beliefs surround eggs at Easter time. In some cultures, it is felt that using eggs cooked on Easter as fertilizer for trees and crops will bring about a good yield. Other lore holds that the yolks of eggs laid on Good Friday and saved for one hundred years would turn to diamonds. An early Christian legend tells that Simon of Cyrene, the man who helped Jesus carry his cross, was an egg peddler. When Simon returned to his eggs after the crucifixion, he found that the eggs had been beautifully decorated.

In some countries, groups of people would pack a picnic of

eggs, then go to the cemetery to share the good news of Easter with all buried there. It is said in Europe that to exchange Easter eggs with your true love means that your love will last until the insides of the egg turn to dust. In Hungary, when a girl gives a red egg to her love he presents her with a bottle of perfume, first sprinkling her with some of it to keep her young and pretty.

Many countries decorate eggs for Easter. Generally, they are hens' eggs, but on occasion other types of eggs are used, especially ostrich, duck, and goose eggs. The people of Poland and the Ukraine decorate eggs using an ancient technique of drawing with wax and dye. These eggs, called *pysanky*, are embellished with many Easter symbols, and are objects of great beauty.

The custom of setting up an Easter egg tree came from Holland, and the first egg tree in the United States is said to have been in Pennsylvania. The Swiss cut a branch from a fruit tree in blossom, bring it inside, and decorate it with blown eggs. Children then walk around the tree, making secret wishes. Swedish children decorate trees with eggs, birds, and candy, as well as witches.

A wonderful custom in many European countries is to cut a branch from a flowering tree and decorate it with ribbons. These branches are then used to give gentle Easter spankings to one another as a sign of good luck and hope for the new season. Children often tap the adults in the family to get treats, and treats are given to prevent being tapped.

Connection

The egg is a wonderful symbol of resurrection. Out of a seemingly dead egg, new life comes. As we pray during this Easter season, perhaps as we enjoy eating a hard-boiled egg, let us reflect on this mystery with words such as these:

Creator God, we see this mystery of death into life in the symbol of an egg. Let us always remember your kindness and generosity, as we enjoy the fruits of Easter, and share in the glory of the risen Christ. Alleluia!

Extension

• Have colored, hard-boiled eggs on hand. With your family or students, decorate the eggs using colored tape, modeling clay, or colored glue. Encourage everyone to use symbols for themselves, such as their initials, or a symbol that might represent an aspect of their personality.

•Visit a cemetery during the Easter season. Bring a few flowers to place on the graves, and remember your forebears in faith, those who helped make you the person you are. Share stories with your children of family members who have died.

•Cut Easter shapes from masking tape, and place on clean, hard-boiled eggs. Dip the eggs in dye until the desired color is achieved. Let dry, then remove the tape. The natural egg color will show in the shape. You can also try different dyeing techniques, making your own natural colors by boiling eggs with onion skins, beets, broccoli, or coffee grounds.

When cooking with eggs during the days before Easter, save the eggshells, wash them, and let them dry. Crush the eggshells, and glue them onto construction paper and the like to make Easter pictures. Color the shells with marker or paint when the glue is dry.

•Here are some egg games that are popular in other countries. Try these at home or in your classroom.

Children in Iran and Iraq hold colored, hard-boiled eggs in their right hands, while they look for others with eggs of the same color as theirs. They then run toward them, and try to break each other's egg. The one who breaks the other's egg goes home with two eggs.

The children of Europe and Australia play a similar game. On Easter Monday, players line up in two rows facing each other. Each person is holding a hard-boiled egg. They race toward players in the other row, trying to break the opponent's egg. The game continues until all the players with unbroken eggs have a chance to challenge all the others with unbroken eggs. The person with the last unbroken egg is the winner.

Collecting the most eggs in an Easter egg hunt is a popular German game. The eggs are placed in rows, one row for each participant. When the signal is given, the participants race down their row collecting the eggs. The first one over the finish line with all of the eggs in the basket is declared the winner.

•Read *The Egg Tree* by Katherine Milhous.

FIRE

Origin

Fire has long been a powerful symbol of Easter. In early Christian times, villages would prepare for the Easter Vigil by extinguishing all house fires as well as all candlesticks and lamps. The boys of the village would then go to the church and build up a pile of logs underneath the Easter fire.

Once the fire was started and blessed, the boys would pull out the lighted logs and bring one to each of the houses in the village. There, all the candles and lamps in the house would be lit with the new fire. Then the log would be put out and saved to be burned in the kitchen stove during a storm to ward off damage.

Fire was used in pagan rituals to welcome the spring. After the fire was lit, there was much dancing and feasting. Traditionally, the first fire of spring was to be lit by the king.

An Irish legend tells of Saint Patrick, who sailed up the River Boyne on the first night of spring, landed, built a huge fire, and lit it. As the flames danced in the dark night, the Irish king happened upon the scene and became very angry. Patrick had lit the fire before the king! Wisely, Patrick told the pagan king the story of the first Easter, which not only abated the king's anger but caused him to convert to Christianity.

In some parts of Austria, fires were lit on mountain peaks just after sunset on Holy Saturday, while musicians paraded through the villages playing religious songs.

Connection

Fire is a mysterious thing. It can burn in places were there is little or no air, or where the materials to burn are not dry. When fire takes hold of something it can burn quickly, causing either good or devastation.

The lighting of the new fire can be a time to reflect on the fire that burns within. What helps us keep the fire of God's life alive within us? What tends to put that fire out? This can be a time to remember the gift of faith that God has given us, and to find ways to nourish the fire of faith.

Extension

•Collect pieces of candle left over from use at parties and other occasions throughout the year. Melt the wax in a double boiler, and shape into a new candle.

•With your students, cover an empty paper towel roll with white paper. Ask each student for the name of one person who has been a light in his or her life, and write down these names on the covered tube. Glue or tape the tube to a piece of cardboard so that it will stand up like a candle. Place this in the center of your classroom, and say a special prayer of thanks for these people.

•During the Easter season, designate one nighttime hour in the evening a week to not use electric lights. Be creative about what can be done while only using natural light. When the lights are turned on, sing a song, such as "You Are the Light of the World."

•Create a Paschal candle for Easter. Take a large white candle. Paint or draw an alpha (A) near the top, and an omega (Ω) near the bottom of the candle. (These are the first and last letters of the Greek alphabet, and are used to remind us that God has no beginning and no end.)

Then, place five cloves, red tacks, or grains of incense in between the alpha and omega to form a cross, one tack at each point and one in the center. These represent the wounds in Jesus' hand, feet, and side. Finally, paint or draw the year on the candle. Light this candle on Holy Saturday evening from the new fire, or on Easter, at your family dinner. Keep the candle in a prominent place throughout the Easter season.

HOLY THURSDAY

Origin

Tradition establishes Holy Thursday as the time when Jesus and the disciples shared the last supper. The Eucharist was instituted at this time, and first offered to the followers of Christ. The sacred time known as the Triduum begins with the liturgy on Holy Thursday evening and ends on the evening of Easter Sunday.

In England, this day is sometimes called "shear Thursday," which comes from the practice of men who sheared their beards in grief at the betrayal of Jesus. Some refer to this day as "clean Thursday," and spend the day doing a thorough housecleaning. In addition, it is sometimes called "kiss Thursday," because of the kiss of Judas.

Several traditions associate the color green with Holy Thursday. There was an old custom of giving people a green branch as a sign that the fast of Lent was over. Penitents who were readmitted into the church on Holy Thursday wore sprigs of green herbs to express their joy, and were referred to as the "green ones." Some people ate only green foods, such as spinach and salads, in the belief that not to do so would make you so unlucky that you could turn into a donkey.

The name "Maundy Thursday" comes from the custom of washing the feet of another, in commemoration of Jesus' action at the last supper. (The word "maundy" comes from *mandatum*, meaning "commandment," and refers to the words Jesus said as he began to wash the feet of his disciples: "A new commandment I give you..." (John 13:34)

Traditionally, English kings and queens would wash the feet of as many people as they were years old. Each person was then given a small purse which held specially minted coins called "maundy money." Although English royals no longer wash people's feet, they give to one old man and one old woman silver coins for each year of the king or queen's age.

One story tells that it was the custom among some people to fully bathe only on Holy Thursday. Since it was once thought that washing all over was dangerous to one's health, a bath on Holy Thursday may have been thought to contain special blessings to maintain health.

Connection

Washing the feet of another is an act of pure humility. But we can practice humility without doing anything that profound. Being humble can simply mean being modest and unpretentious.

We show humility when we give others credit for their accomplishments and their good deeds, when we recognize that they have succeeded, and when we are excited that someone has done something fulfilling to them. Further, we can be humble by ignoring the shortcomings and mistakes of another. We don't have to wash their feet, but we can cleanse the judgments that we make about them.

Extension

•On Holy Thursday, wear something green. Let it remind you of mourning as well as the newness of spring, and the upcoming death and resurrection of Jesus.

•Make maundy purses, and place special messages or items in them to give to others.

•Attend a Holy Thursday ritual where the Last Supper is re-enacted, and offer to be one of the participants.

•Give bread to those who may be hungry, through a food bank or homeless shelter.

•As you bathe, take time to say a prayer of healing.

•Read "Out, Witch, Out!" from *Pancakes and Painted Eggs* by Jean Chapman.

HOLY WEEK

Origin

Holy Week traditions are common throughout many countries. The Germans call Holy Week "silent week," setting it apart as a time for prayer and reflection. In Finland, each day of Holy Week has a special name: stocking Sunday, beam Monday, splinter Tuesday, bell Wednesday, evil spirit Thursday, long Friday, and yarn Saturday. We can imagine the types of activities that happen on each of these days!

In South American countries, there are parades on each day of Holy Week. Early on Good Friday morning, the people parade through the dark streets, as drums beat and church bells slowly ring. Some carry large statues of Jesus and Mary, while others carry candles to brighten the darkness as they sing sad songs.

Several Holy Week customs revolve around Judas. In some places, the Wednesday of Holy Week is called "spy Wednesday" because this is believed to have been the day on which Judas made his deal with the high priests. In Portugal, Sicily, and Spain an effigy of Judas is burned on Good Friday, and in Mexico, a papier-mâché image of Judas is burned on Holy Saturday. Pottery would often be broken on Good Friday, so that every piece with its jagged edges would bruise Judas.

For many years, Good Friday was called "God's Friday." In some countries it is still called "big Friday," "Holy Friday," or "silent Friday." In parts of southern England, Good Friday was sometimes called "marble day," to note the closing of marble-playing season which began on Ash Wednesday. In other parts of England, Good Friday was also called "long rope day," as people took the ropes out of the fishing boats and jumped rope.

Connection

We have all hurt another through words or actions, or through our omissions of doing something good. Then, there are the times when we show our love for ourselves, but do not treat others with love as Jesus commanded. When we do show love, what is our motive? Are we acting out of love of God and others, or out of the benefit we can get from our action? Jesus calls us to kindness, love, and caring concern toward God, other persons, and ourselves. Let us examine our motives during this Holy Week, to make sure that we are on the right track.

Extension

•Marbles can remind us of the soldiers who rolled dice to get Jesus' garments after the crucifixion. Place some marbles in a glass container, and put these in a prominent spot on Good Friday to remember this aspect of Jesus' passion.

•Write a letter, as a family or class, to someone who is in prison. (Contact the diocesan prison ministry for suggestions.) Tell the person that you will pray for him or her. Perhaps you can send along a small token, such as a book or prayer card.

•On Wednesday of Holy Week, pray for those who, like Judas, betray others with their words or deeds. Also, pray for those who have been betrayed.

•Put a purple cloth over the television set on Friday (or throughout Holy Week, if you can), to keep silence and a prayerful atmosphere in your home during this time.

• Break a small clay flower pot. On each piece write an evil in the world that you will work to improve.

•Name the days of Holy Week according to your interests and needs. Perform a special action that fits the name.

HOT CROSS BUNS

Origin

Each spring, the early pagan people would make wheat cakes to honor Eastre, the goddess of spring. When Christian people adopted this custom, they cut a cross into the buns before they were baked. And since these cakes were best enjoyed hot out of the oven, they became known as hot cross buns.

Hot cross buns are a traditional Good Friday food. Today, however, they are also made on Ash Wednesday, and can often be found in bakeries all during Lent.

One legend connected with these buns tells of a monk who was disturbed by all of the poor families living in England. Being a baker by trade, he decided to make buns that could be given to the poor so they would not go hungry. To make them delicious as well, the monk filled them with raisins and spices.

After they had baked, the monk put a frosting cross on the buns, then took them out to share with the poor. One young boy offered to take some of the buns and sell them to make money for the poor. It was said that the boy would run through the streets of the village, singing:

Hot cross buns! Hot cross buns!
One a penny, two a penny, hot cross buns!
If you have no daughters, give them to your sons.
One a penny, two a penny, hot cross buns.

Several customs involve hot cross buns. One is to hang a bun from the ceiling of the house to protect the house and to bring good luck. Another is to grind dried hot cross buns into powder to use for medicinal purposes, or to sprinkle on fields in hope of a good yield. Bread bakers often cut a cross in the bun dough before it begins to rise, to release the gasses of the yeast. However, some bakers also do this as a blessing upon the bread.

Connection

Bread, of which buns are a type, is a simple, everyday food.

Likewise, living a Christian life happens through the events of everyday life. The simple acts of kindness, such as a friendly greeting, a courteous gesture, or a listening ear, are things we can do everyday. A sincere smile is another simple gesture. Smiles tend to be contagious; should we not be happy as Christians and be willing to share that joy?

Extension

• This activity can be done on Ash Wednesday, Good Friday, or on another more convenient day during Lent. Purchase frozen bread dough, defrost, and shape into buns. (You can also make a sweet dough from a bread machine mix or other bread recipe.) Allow the dough to rise as directed on the package.

Before baking, take a sharp knife and cut a cross in each bun. After the buns are baked, make a simple frosting from confectioners sugar, and use this to place a cross on the top of each bun. Share the hot cross buns with your family or students, or bring them to a food pantry to share with the hungry.

• At a family meal or during a class, take a piece of bread or roll and share it with all gathered as a sign of unity, in remembrance of Jesus, the bread of life.

• Take some time to get to know someone who seems different from you. Learn to appreciate their gifts and talents.

LILY

Origin

The lily is called the angel of flowers, because of its beauty and goodness. Most Christians are familiar with Jesus' words to his disciples: "Consider the lilies of the field; they neither toil nor reap, yet not even Solomon in all his glory is arrayed like one of these" (Matthew 6:29 and Luke 12:27–28).

White lilies are a popular representation of the meaning of Easter. The white symbolizes purity and joy, indicative of the resurrection. Its petals flare out like the bell of a trumpet, suggesting Gabriel's horn as it blows a welcome to spring. The lily bulb itself is buried in fall, and grows each spring from below the ground, just as Jesus was buried in the tomb and rose triumphant into life.

This white, ornamental lily, native to the small islands south of Japan, became associated with Easter during the last century. The sand dollar has markings similiar to an Easter lily, with a star in the middle and five nail holes on the side. When the sand dollar is broken open, five white doves "appear," symbolizing peace.

During the Middle Ages, it was common to associate the lily with Mary, and many legends grew up around this. In many places, the common name for the Easter lily is the "Madonna lily," in reference to the Blessed Mother. Further, the lily of the valley is said to have sprung from the tears of Mary as she wept at the foot of the cross.

Connection

The lily is a natural masterpiece of God's beauty. Yet in order for it to grow it must be buried in the darkness of the earth and receive the right amount of light and water. All of us have "bulbs" that we keep buried from other people, perhaps even hidden from ourselves. We might have buried the bulbs of a grudge or resentment toward someone, of mistreating the environment, or of being possessive of our talents and gifts.

Just as a flower bulb struggles to break through the ground, it is likewise hard for us to break away and let go of our hidden bulbs. Yet we know that God calls us to growth and rebirth. We are fully human only when we nurture our bulbs to health and share the goodness that God has stored in us.

Extension

•Give a lily plant to someone who is housebound or sick at Easter. Share with them its symbolism of rebirth and resurrection.

•When the lilies that decorated your home or church die after Easter, take the bulbs from the lilies, put them in a brown paper bag, and store in a cool, dry place. In the fall, plant these bulbs so that they can bloom once again the following spring.

•Sometime during the lenten season, donate money to a funeral home so that they can buy a lily for a needy person who dies during the Easter season.

•Examine a sand dollar and reflect on its Christian symbolism.

•Find food for thought in Hosea 14:6. Also, read one of the scripture passages about lilies cited in the "Origin" section.

MARDI GRAS

Origin

Mardi Gras means "Fat Tuesday" in French, while "carnival" is derived from a Latin term meaning "farewell to meat." The phrase "fat Tuesday" could have evolved from the French custom of having a fat ox lead the carnival procession on the day before Lent began. Or, it may have been used to refer to the fact that all the food left over from winter storage had to be eaten by Ash Wednesday.

In the early Middle Ages, the Mardi Gras celebration often began as early as the feast of the Epiphany (January 6). These original carnivals frequently lasted for as long a period of time as the lenten season itself. Eventually, carnival was shortened to the ten days before Ash Wednesday, ending on Fat Tuesday.

Mardi Gras celebrations often include elaborate costumes and parades, and festivities earmarked by revelry and chaos. Some see Mardi Gras as a commemoration of our dark sides, and a cry back to primitive rites of renewal. Indeed, Mardi Gras and New Year's Eve celebrations are very much alike in spirit as well as in practice, perhaps owing to the fact that the new year once began in March, right before the start of spring.

Connection
In the spirit of Mardi Gras, reflect on what makes you laugh. Are the jokes you hear and repeat in line with Christian values? Are they at the expense of another person, ethnic group, or gender? What about the magazines, television shows, movies, or music that you enjoy? Imagine Jesus sitting beside you while you read, watch, or listen: would he find the same things amusing that you do?

Extension
•In your home or classroom, celebrate Fat Tuesday with a party. Decorate the room with crepe paper streamers and balloons. Play games and share favorite foods and sweets. Place pussy willows and forsythia branches in water to show the promise of spring.

•Select a favorite food from the refrigerator or cupboard, and consume all of it before Ash Wednesday. Do not purchase any more of this food until after Easter.

•Share a few jokes or funny stories with someone, and ask if they have anything funny to share with you.

•Review the printed materials you read regularly, as well as your choices of TV shows, movies, and music. With family members or your students, state your opinion of popular but inappropriate materials. Write and share your views with those responsible for producing the content of these media.

NEW CLOTHES

Origin
Spring is a time for all creation to put on new life. The buds that have been wrapped in their winter covers come forth, ready to bloom. Animals shed their winter coats to prepare for the warmth of the new season. People who live in climates with cold winters begin to put away their

heavy clothing to make room for the less cumbersome clothing of spring.

Easter is a day to wear new clothes. Even if one cannot get an entire outfit, a new pair of gloves or socks is enough. New clothes represent the new life given to us through the death and resurrection of Jesus. It is a time to take off the old and put on the new.

At one time, the new year began in March, and people would wear new clothes to mark the beginning of the year. They wanted to wear new or different clothing because they wanted to be as beautiful as the earth that was blossoming with flowers and greenery. When the Julian calendar was put into popular use, Easter would often fall in or near March, so the custom of wearing new clothes at this time became connected to Easter.

For Christians, wearing new clothes links the assembly to the catechumens who are baptized at the Easter Vigil. These new Christians were traditionally robed in white garments to symbolize their new life in Christ. The custom of an Easter parade can be traced back to King Constantine, who asked the people of his kingdom to dress in their best clothes and stroll about the countryside in honor of Jesus.

Connection

Winter is long and dark. As spring comes, all of nature begins to put on new clothes, breaking out of the shells and seed coats of winter. What are some things that could be changed in our lives to make the coming of spring a celebration of new life?

Extension

•Try making Easter bonnets with your family or students. These can be made from plain hats you may have on hand, or simple felt and straw hats purchased for the occasion. Decorate with ribbons, flowers, and other signs of spring. (Boys might want to decorate their baseball caps.) Wear the hats on Easter Sunday, and have a parade to show off your creations.

•Consider shopping at a secondhand store for an Easter outfit. This can be a gesture of respect for the earth, by reusing items in good condition.

•Ritualize the letting go of winter by writing down or illustrating things in your life that you would like to let die. (This can be thoughts, ideas, attitudes, material items, or behaviors). Dig a large hole, and place the papers at the bottom. Then plant some seeds on top or an outdoor plant to symbolize growth and new life.

•When taking out spring clothes and packing away winter ones, see if there are any clothes in good shape that can be donated to a secondhand store.

•Plan to wear something white on Easter as a sign of baptism and new life. Say a prayer of thanksgiving for the gift of faith.

PALM SUNDAY

Origin

Palm Sunday celebrations can be traced back to Italy, starting around the 8th century. Tradition associates palms with the biblical account of Jesus' ride into Jerusalem prior to the crucifixion.

In pre-Christian times, palms were thought to ward off evil, storms, and lightning. Over the centuries, Jews, Christians, and Muslims have held processions to the local cemetery to place palm branches on the graves as a promise of resurrection and symbol of new life.

Palms are blessed and distributed as part of Christian liturgical worship on the Sunday before Easter. When palms are not available, however, branches of other trees are used in their place. Thus, Palm Sunday is sometimes called Olive Sunday or Branch Sunday; in England, it is called Sunday of the Willow Boughs, and in Germany, Blossom Sunday.

Blessed palms can be used for home decorations. Often the palms are hung near the family cross or on the front door. A bundle of branches can be gathered at the bottom like a tall bouquet, as people do in Guatemala. German people use palm trees decorated with ribbons and flowers to beautify their homes.

In Austria, Bavaria, and the Slavic countries, farmers and their families walk through their fields and buildings on the afternoon of Palm Sunday. They pray and sing, while placing a sprig of blessed palm in each pasture, as well as in every barn and stable. This gesture is believed to ward off the punishments of weather, disease, or tragedy, and to draw God's blessings on the year's harvest.

Older people sometimes refer to Palm Sunday as Fig Sunday. This comes from a bygone practice of eating figs or fig pudding at the midday meal on the Sunday before Easter. Children would be given packets of figs and told to remember the parable of the barren fig tree.

Palm Sunday is called Willow Sunday in some parts of the world. The willow tree is one of the first plants to spring into bloom after the long winter, and its branches have been called the "rod of life" and the "stroke of health."

In England and Russia, pussy willow branches are given out on the Sunday before Easter, and people tap each other with them for good luck, saying, "Be as tall as the willow, healthy as water, and rich as the earth."

An old English custom is to distribute "pax cakes" on Palm Sunday. Tradition tells that a woman in Heresfordshire, England, set aside money so that ale and cakes could be given to all the members of her parish on Palm Sunday. She felt that those who shared food together as community might be more willing to reconcile their differences, and thereby make their Easter celebration more worthy.

The pax cakes, eventually marked with a lamb and flag, would be given out by the priest at the end of the Palm Sunday liturgy, with the greeting "God and good neighborhood." Then, the pax cakes would be eaten and enjoyed. The custom evolved to include anyone who had quarreled during the year the opportunity to share a pax cake and resolve their differences.

Connection

Palm Sunday is a time for peace and reconciliation. This might be needed within oneself, with another family member, a neighbor or friend, a member of your parish, or a coworker. We might also be called to bring peace to criminals or addicts, all of whom can cause harm and injury to themselves or others. Let us make a gesture of forgiveness and acceptance to someone with whom there is dissension, and allow God an opening into our hearts.

Extension

•Place a piece of palm from church in each room of your house, or in your classroom, and pray for God's blessing in the coming year.

•Take a Palm Sunday walk and remember Jesus' walk to Jerusalem. Look for signs of spring, such as pussy willows and spring flowers.

•Gently tap others with a green branch, a pussy willow, or a palm, and wish them good health by saying, "Be as tall as the willow, healthy as water, and rich as the earth."

•Visit the cemetery and put flowers or palm branches on the grave of a loved one, as well as of a person whose grave appears ignored.

•Give a pax cake to someone with whom you have had a struggle during the past year. (Any cake can be used for a pax cake.) Share the story of how the pax cake custom originated, then try to reconcile your differences with the other person.

•With your family or students, read the Palm Sunday story from Scripture. You can find this in the following gospels, starting with the verses noted here: Luke 19:28, John 12:12, or Mark 11:1.

PIGS

Origin

The pig was a symbol of good luck and prosperity among the European Christians. German men sometimes wore little figures of pigs on their watch chains as good luck charms. To wish another good luck, they might say "have a pig." Owning a pig was also considered good luck, and in Hungary, the ace in a deck of cards was called the "pig."

This symbolism of good luck and prosperity carried over into the use of piggy banks. At Christmas time in medieval England, merchants gave money boxes, shaped like pigs and containing coins, to their apprentices. During Lent, piggy banks were often used as "mite boxes" or "alms boxes," to collect money for the poor. Since at one time Christians could not eat meat on any day during Lent, the clay pig reminded the family of Easter ham and sausage.

The custom of eating of ham on Easter Sunday may have come from a practice in early England, where Christians would eat bacon to show contempt for the Jewish practice of abstaining from pork. When William the Conqueror ascended the throne, and preferred ham to bacon, his taste became custom and the prejudicial motive was eliminated.

Connection

Every part of the pig is used for food or other products; it is said that we use everything but the "squeak" of pigs. Each of us has many talents and gifts that can be used to benefit others. Yet do we offer every bit of ourselves to further the presence of God? Are we fully engrossed in the work of God, regardless of how dirty we might get or what others' opinions of us might be?

Extension

• In your home or classroom, set up a piggy bank that will be used throughout Lent as a way to put aside money for the poor. Contributions to a piggy bank should come from a denial of something, rather than from excess money.

Some ways to collect money are to put aside a certain amount of money each day; donate the amount of a certain product, like a candy bar, snack food, or beverage; contribute the cost of a meal out; or give a percentage of each person's allowance or weekly paycheck.

• Find a ceramic or clay piggy bank that can be sealed during Lent, then broken in order to give away the money inside. The ritual of opening the bank can symbolize the breaking of our attachment to material goods, then sharing those goods with the less fortunate.

If you chose a piggy bank that can be reused, store it away after Lent to take out and use next year. This will create a special aura and significance about the meaning of the piggy bank.

• Donate an Easter ham to a food bank or needy family.

PRETZELS

Origin

Pretzels been around since the time of the Roman Empire. Because they are made from a mixture of flour, salt, and water, pretzels were considered an ideal lenten food.

Pretzels are said to have been first made by monks, who twisted long, thin strips of dough into a shape that looked like praying arms. Thus, pretzels were first called *bracellae*, or "little arms." Some traditions say that the small twist in the middle of the pretzel represents a child's arms, while the encircling part of the pretzel is the parent's arms. The three holes formed with this type of twist represent the Trinity.

For a long time, pretzels were considered strictly lenten fare. In some cities, pretzels were distributed to the poor during Lent. In other places, pretzels were sold by street vendors, and eaten with beer or soup. In Austria, pretzels were suspended from palm branches on Palm Sunday, for passersby to pluck and eat.

Connection

Pretzels come in many shapes and have very simple ingredients. The ingredients of pretzels are ones that are easily found and yet have a story far beyond what we see. People are often the same way. Frequently we look only at the outside and fail to see who they are beyond their surface appearance.

Extension

•Use this prayer as grace before the beginning of your main meal each day during Lent. A pretzel could also be placed on each person's plate as a reminder of the lenten season.

Gracious God, thank you for giving us Jesus to show us the way. Help us to remember that Jesus gave his life for us. Help us to give of ourselves to others during this season of Lent. We ask this in Jesus' name. Amen.

You can also use this prayer to start your religious education classes during Lent, giving out a pretzel to each student before or after class.

•Make pretzels with your family or class during the week before Ash Wednesday. Here is a simple recipe:

1 1/2 cups warm water
1 package active dry yeast
1/2 teaspoon sugar
1/2 teaspoon salt
4 1/2 to 5 cups flour
1 egg beaten for glazing (optional)
coarse salt

Place warm water in a bowl. Sprinkle yeast, sugar, and salt into the water and dissolve. Mix flour into the water mixture to form a soft ball. Take the dough, place it on a floured board, and knead it for a few minutes. Let rest for about one hour.

Roll into a rectangle about 1/2 inch thick and about 6 inches long. Cut the dough into 1/4 inch strips. Twist them into a pretzel shape. Place the pretzels on a cookie sheet, brush with beaten egg, and sprinkle with coarse salt. Bake at 425 degrees for between 12 and 15 minutes.

•Use a reflection on pretzels as the basis for prayer in a scripture study group. Reflect on each ingredient as it is added to the bowl for mixing:

—water, to start the dough;
—yeast, to give lightness to the dough;
—sugar, to feed the yeast and add sweetness;
—salt, the spice of life, to give flavor;
—flour, to add substance to the dough.

How do each of these ingredients echo our lives in faith?

•Shellac pretzels to make them waterproof. Place a string on each pretzel and attach a piece of paper with the story of pretzels on it. Give them away on Ash Wednesday. Invite people to hang the pretzel near the door of their home all during Lent as a reminder to pray and do good works during Lent.

•Pack a pretzel in your lunch each day during Lent.

PURPLE CLOTH

Origin

The custom of hanging a large piece of purple or white fabric in front of the sanctuary
was begun around the 11th century, and
practiced in England, France, and
Germany. It is thought that the more recent
practice of covering statues with purple
cloth during Lent may have evolved from
this ancient tradition.

    This cloth, decorated with crosses, was
sometimes called the "hunger cloth," and separated the penitents
from seeing the altar during the lenten season. During the main
parts of the Mass it would be pulled away so that the altar could
be seen, but immediately after Mass, the cloth would be let down
again. It was finally removed on the Wednesday of Holy Week.

Connection

The purple cloth used during Lent was a physical divider to separate the penitents from the other parish members. We, too, can
have dividers between us and others, as well as between us and
God. These can separate us from the love of God and others.

    Other dividers can be positive. They can separate us from the
frantic pace of every day, from the noises that take up our attention, and from excessive demands on our time and energy. In order
to listen to God, we must deliberately shut out our environment,
and have a time of quiet and calm. It is through moments of quiet
that our relationship with God is cultivated.

Extension

    •During Lent, drape a piece of purple fabric over a table or
chair in your house or meeting area. Use it as a reminder of the
season, and change the cloth to white for Easter.

    •Hang a piece of purple cloth over the crucifixes in your home
or classroom during Lent, to remind your family and students that
this is a time of renewal.

•Wear a purple ribbon on your lapel or wrist during Lent as a witness to your belief in the death and resurrection of Jesus. Put a purple button in your coin purse or change pocket as a reminder of the need to change during the season of Lent.

RABBITS

Origin

According to pagan history, rabbits were the favorite animal of Eastre, the goddess of spring. She was thought to have placed eggs in the tall grass at the start of spring, and use rabbits to deliver the eggs to children.

Besides the pagan tradition, several other factors contribute to rabbits being seen as an Easter symbol: they are extremely fertile animals, thus potent signs of abundant new life; they sometimes represent the moon, which relates to Easter's date being set by the moon; finally, rabbits burrow under ground, which is likened to Jesus in the tomb.

When the German people came to the United States, they brought with them the legend of a poor woman who always wanted to surprise children. One year, the woman had no money to buy gifts for the children. So she dyed all sorts of eggs in rainbow colors, and hid them in nests made of grass and sticks. Just as the children approached the nests, a rabbit hopped away. The children then believed that the rabbit had left the eggs as an Easter surprise.

Connection

Rabbits are a sign of new life, a powerful Easter metaphor. We, too, can produce new life through our Christian thoughts and actions. Like rabbits, we can create new life by doing random acts of kindness, and good deeds for others. Actions might be as ordinary as giving someone a thank you, a compliment, a smile, or a kind gesture. These simple actions could motivate the receiver to do the same for someone else.

Rabbits can reproduce every 30 days. It is possible that our acts of thoughtfulness can reproduce new life in a matter of minutes. What joy to know that we, by our thoughtful behavior, could be the catalysts for many more kind words, thoughts, and actions!

Extension

•On Good Friday, to represent the death of Jesus, place a rabbit figure under a container or in a box, and put it in a conspicuous location. On Easter Sunday morning, take the rabbit out of the container and sing an Easter song or an Alleluia.

•Plan to do random and secret acts of kindness, perhaps every day for one week, or each Wednesday during Lent.

•At home or in class, make bunnies out of marshmallows and toothpicks.

•With your family or students, read aloud *The Velveteen Rabbit*, by Margery Williams.

•Take a walk outside, and look for signs of new life. Thank God for the budding trees, newly started grass, hints of flowers, or the longer hours of daylight.

SHROVE TUESDAY

Origin

Shrove Tuesday is the day before Ash Wednesday. To "shrive" means to confess one's sins, or to have one's sins absolved. The name "Shrove Tuesday" is said to have come from the custom of ringing the "shriving bell" on the day before Lent, to summon the people to church to be "shriven," that is, to confess their sins, at the beginning of Lent.

This day is also known by many other names, most of which

reflect regional customs and practices: Carnival, Fat Tuesday, Mardi Gras, *Fastnacht* (eve of the fast), or Doughnut Tuesday. On this day, families would often eat pancakes and fried doughnuts to use up the butter, eggs, and dairy products that were left behind from winter, and which could not be eaten during Lent. In some traditions, people would prepare for Lent by putting away knick-knacks and beginning their spring cleaning.

In England, Shrove Tuesday was called Pancake Tuesday. On this day, each town would hold a pancake race. The women of the village would meet at the town square with a pan of pancakes. They would then run toward the church, tossing their pancakes three times into the air. When they arrived at the church, the bell ringer would get a kiss from the winner, as well as all the pancakes.

There was a time when English children went from door to door on Shrove Tuesday, asking for treats and chanting rhymes such as:

Pancakes! Pancakes! Pancake day!

If you don't give us any, we'll all run away.

One custom popular today on Shrove Tuesday is to make gaily colored paper or cloth banners with words on them, such as "Alleluia!" "New life," or "Joy." These banners can be hung for a Mardi Gras party, then "buried" in a box and hidden until they are "resurrected" on Easter morning. Another common practice is still to have pancakes on Shrove Tuesday, along with rich party foods.

Connection

In the United States, fasting from certain or all food is a familiar way to express an opinion, to make a political point, or to state opposition to something. It is commonly associated with spiritual preparation during Lent.

Another way to mark Lent can be through "visual fasting." Sight is a means of gathering information, some of which contributes to our spiritual growth, while some does not. Our visual fasting might be to refrain from making negative judgments about others, based on their appearance. Or, we can put away knick-knacks or some other pleasing decorations during Lent.

Extension

•Eat pancakes on Tuesdays throughout Lent. Put the equivalent of the money you save with this simple meal in your mite box.

•With your family or students, read aloud the traditional story, "The Little Red Hen." Then talk about people who may have asked for help during the day. Have each person reflect on why they did or did not help when asked.

•Offer a smile and warm greeting to a person that you usually criticize or regard with dislike.

•Visually fast by putting away a favorite knickknack or decoration, and leaving the space open.

•Volunteer to help spring clean a public space, for example, a park, building, or street.

•Fast from a certain food throughout Lent, and donate containers of that food to a food pantry or soup kitchen.

STATIONS OF THE CROSS

Origin

The stations of the cross, sometimes called the "way of the cross," have a long history. This form of devotion began at the time of the crusades, and, in recreating Jesus' passion and death, was a way to bring events in the Holy Land closer to Europe.

The traditional stations have fourteen scenes, each one commemorating a part of Jesus' last day on earth. Those praying the way of the cross follow each station by offering a brief reflection and prayer at each scene.

In the Middle Ages, only the monks and members of the royal class knew how to read. Practices such as the Jesse tree and the stations of the cross were used to teach the Bible to the commoners, who could not read.

Over the years, the Franciscan fathers have maintained as shrines the places in the Holy Land that mark the events of Jesus' passion and death. Even today, many people make a pilgrimage to these sites.

Particularly in Mexico and South America, people reenact the stations on Good Friday, in the form of a passion play. In India, it is the custom to carry statues of Mary and Jesus from opposite ends of the town until the two meet. There, a prayer is said and the statues are taken into the church.

Connection

Often in our lives, there are many times that there is suffering. These times give us a chance to relate our own pain and suffering to Jesus' passion. If we turn to Jesus as our example, and reflect on our troubles one at a time, we can find strength and build a stronger relationship with God.

Jesus did not walk to the cross alone, even though many of his friends ran away in fear. He had the support of many women who had been part of his life, as well as strangers along the way. When life seems difficult it is good to know that there are people who can help us with our journey.

Extension

•With your family or class, pray the stations of the cross. (You can find booklets at your parish, or at a nearby Christian bookstore, or see the "Suggested Resources" at the back of this book.) Give each member of the group a station to reflect on (if the group is small, give people more than one station). Encourage people to make the reflections personal, finding a way to relate a difficulty in life to Jesus' passion.

•Make fourteen large crosses from cardboard or heavy paper. Then, find pictures from the newspaper or from magazines that can be used to represent each one of the stations. Cut out the pictures, and glue them to the crosses. Use these on Good Friday to make a way of the cross, or at another convenient time during Lent.

•As a group, reflect on the traditional stations. Then talk about how to write contemporary stations, thinking of the sufferings of people in today's world. You could then use these stations for Good Friday, along with the crosses made as above.

•Volunteer at a homeless shelter, battered women's shelter, soup kitchen, or other type of service agency to better understand some of the hardships people live with every day. Find some way that your family or students can help alleviate this suffering.

WATER

Origin

Water has long been a symbol of new life, health, and fertility, and has been used in rituals and blessings since recorded time. Ancient peoples poured water over animals to keep them healthy, and over crops to make them grow tall. Friends and families sprinkled each other with water, while giving wishes for health, good luck, and a long life.

By the Middle Ages, many Easter customs developed around water. In Eastern Europe and France, it was believed that if a girl washed her face in a running brook on Easter, she would receive many blessings, and have special gifts and powers for the year. Another Easter custom was for the boys of a village to sprinkle the girls with water to bring them fertility and health.

Other people bottled water from a nearby river on Easter Sunday and kept it until the following Easter. This would be used to heal wounds and cure illnesses. The Irish gathered water on Easter to protect themselves from witches and other evil spirits.

The sprinkling rite has became an important part of both the Easter Vigil and Easter Sunday liturgies. At this time, baptismal vows are renewed, and the priest walks throughout the congregation sprinkling those gathered with water as a reminder of their baptism. This ritual may have originated when people were buried within the walls of the church, and their graves would be blessed by sprinkling water over them.

Also at Easter Vigil on Holy Saturday, the Easter water is blessed, and the candle lit from the new fire is plunged into this Easter water. The assembly is then sprinkled with the new water, and a prayer of blessing in celebration of new life is offered. Blessed water is also used at baptism. Fresh clear water is placed in the baptismal font. Ancient blessings are prayed over the water.

Connection

Water is a source of life. It cleans and refreshes, and keeps us growing: without water, all living things die. But we must also take care of our water and treat it with respect, being careful of what we put in it. Is this not true of our lives, as well? We need to nurture life with work and recreation, time for reading, time for prayer, time to simply be. Let us reflect on some of the ways that we can care for our lives.

Extension

• As a group, experiment with the effects of water on plants. Place two plants in a sunny place. Water one of them regularly, and let the other go without water. Observe how the two plants respond. Reflect on this experiment in light of our baptism.

• Use a sprinkling rite as grace before a family meal, or as part of a prayer before a class or parish meeting. Take a branch from an evergreen tree, dip it in holy water and sprinkle over all gathered, saying: *By the waters of baptism, we are one in Christ.*

• Place a holy water font by the main door of your house. Encourage family members to use this to bless themselves upon entering and leaving the house, as a reminder of our baptism (Most churches have a supply of holy water available to parishioners.)

• Place a bowl of water in the middle of the table on Easter Sunday. Bring out your children's baptismal candles and place them around the bowl as a sign of new life through this sacrament. Then, during the Easter season, float spring flowers in the bowl as a reminder of new life.

SUGGESTED RESOURCES

Bradner, John. *Symbols of Church Seasons and Days.* Ridgefield, CT: Morehouse Publishing Company, 1977.

Bragdon, Allen D. *Joy Through the World.* New York: Dodd, Mead and Company, 1985.

Chapman, Jean. *Pancakes and Painted Eggs.* Chicago: Children's Press International, 1981.

Chesto, Kathleen. *Family Prayer for Family Times: Traditions, Celebrations, and Rituals.* Mystic, CT: Twenty-Third Publications, 1995.

de Paola, Tomie. *The Legend of Old Befana.* New York: Harcourt, Brace, Jovanovich, 1980.

Dues, Greg. *Catholic Customs and Traditions.* Mystic, CT: Twenty-Third Publications, 1992.

Elbert,Virginia Fowler. *Christmas Crafts and Customs Around the World.* Englewood Cliffs, NJ: Prentice Hall, 1984.

Geraghty, Sheila and Kielly, Shiela. *Something Out of the Ordinary: Creative Activities for Religious Education.* Dubuque, IA: Brown–ROA Publishing, 1991.

Geraghty, Sheila and Kielly, Shiela. *Something Out of the Ordinary: 50 Nifty Activities for Review, Reinforcement, and Enrichment.* Dubuque, IA: Brown–ROA Publishing, 1992.

Harper, Howard V. *Days and Customs of All Faiths.* Detroit, MI: Omnigraphics, Inc., 1990.

Hays, Edward. *Prayers for the Domestic Church: A Handbook for Worship in the Home.* Leavenworth, KS: Forest of Peace Books, 1989.

Hays, Edward. *The Quest for the Flaming Pearl.* Leavenworth, KS: Forest of Peace Books, 1994.

Hottes, Alfred Carl. *1001 Christmas Facts and Fancies.* Detroit, MI: Omnigraphics, Inc., 1990.

Hynes, Mary Ellen. *Companion to the Calendar.* Chicago: Liturgy Training Publications, 1993.

Kalman, Bobbie. *We Celebrate Easter.* New York: Crabtree Publishing, 1985.

Lord, Priscilla Sawyer & Foley, Daniel J. *Easter the World Over.* Philadelphia: Chilton Books, 1971.

Milhous, Katherine. *The Egg Tree.* New York: Macmillan Children's Book Group, 1971.

Morris, Ann. *Bread, Bread, Bread.* New York: William Morrow & Company, Inc., 1993.

Myers, Robert J. *Celebrations: The Complete Book of American Holidays.* New York: Doubleday & Co., 1972.

National Conference of Catholic Bishops. *Catholic Household Blessings and Prayers.* Washington, DC: United States Catholic Conference, Inc., 1988.

O'Neal, Debbie Trafton. *Before and After Christmas: Activities and Ideas for Advent and Epiphany.* Minneapolis, MN: Augsburg Press, 1991.

O'Neal, Debbie Trafton. *Before and After Easter.* Minneapolis, MN: Augsburg Press, 1992.

Palangi, Paula. *The Last Straw.* Elgin, IL: David C. Cook, 1992.

Pappas, Lou Seibert. *Bread Baking.* San Leandro, CA: Bristol Publishing Enterprises, Inc., 1992.

Paulus, Trina. *Hope for the Flowers.* Mahwah, NJ: Paulist Press, 1992.

Richardson I.M. *Story of the Christmas Rose.* Mahwah, N.J: Troll Associates, 1988.

Sandak, Cass R. *Easter.* New York: Macmillan Children's Book Group, 1990.

Silverstein, Shel. *The Giving Tree.* New York: HarperCollins, 1964.

Tudor, Tasha. *Take Joy: The Tasha Tudor Christmas Book*. New York: Putnam Publishing Group, 1980.

Tuleja, Thaddeus. *Curious Customs. The Stories Behind More Than 300 Popular American Rituals*. New York: Crown Publishing Group, 1987.

Vaughn, Mary Ann Woloch. *Ukrainian Easter*. Munster, ID: Ukrainian Heritage Company, 1983.

Weiser, Francis X. *The Christmas Book*. Detroit, MI: Omnigraphics, Inc., 1990.

Williams, Margery. *The Velveteen Rabbit*. New York: Avon Books, 1992.

Yolen, Jane. *Hark! A Christmas Sampler*. New York: Putnam Publishing Group, 1991.

Twenty-Third Publications in Mystic, CT has an extensive line of Way of the Cross booklets that are useful for the home or in the classroom. You can order any of these booklets by calling 1-800-321-0411.

Abajian, Diane. *Praying and Doing the Stations of the Cross with Children*. 1980. (Ages 4-7)

Costello, Gwen. *A Bible Way of the Cross for Children*. 1987. (Ages 7-12)

Costello, Gwen. *Stations of the Cross for Teenagers*. 1988. (Ages 12-18)

Huebsch, Bill. *The New Scripture Way of the Cross*. 1992.

Jones, Sue. *The Way of the Cross for Parents*. 1995.

McCann, Deborah. *A Mother's Way of the Cross*. 1990.

Of Related Interest. . .

Advent Stories and Activities
Meeting Jesus through the Jesse Tree
Anne E. Neuberger

Offers 24 ancient stories and symbols (from creation to the nativity) to mark the days before Christmas. Introduces children (7-12) to the tradition of keeping a Jesse Tree with easy-to-follow directions for creating seven types of trees to accommodate various settings, time constraints, and abilities.

ISBN: 0-89622-734-0, 96 pages, $12.95 (order B-22)

Classroom Prayer Services for the Days of Advent and Lent
Gwen Costello

These 60 creative services involve children (7-12) in celebrating God's presence through processions, veneration of the Bible, prayer patterns, speaking parts, guided meditations, and blessings. Catholic customs are also presented. Easily incorporated into lesson plans.

ISBN: 0-89622-737-5, 144 pages, $12.95 (order B-39)

Make Family Time Prime Time
Fun Ways to Build Faith in Your Family
Denise Yribarren and DeAnn Koestner

Provides creative ways for families to engage in spending quality time together through easy to duplicate ideas, activities, games, crafts, recipes, and rituals. Perfect for holy days and holidays as well as for the everyday, mundane times.

ISBN: 0-89622-712-X, 112 pages, $12.95 (order B-32)

Available at religious bookstores or from:

XXIII TWENTY-THIRD PUBLICATIONS
P.O. Box 180 • Mystic, CT 06355
1-800-321-0411
E-Mail:ttpubs@aol.com